CW01508393

Purple into Gold

Purple into Gold

A JOURNEY OF HOPE AND HEALING

CHARMAINE HOST

This edition produced in Great Britain in 2023

Copyright © Charmaine Host 2023

The stories in this book reflect the author's recollection of events. Some names, locations, and identifying characteristics have been changed to protect the privacy of those depicted. Dialogue has been re-created from memory.

Charmaine Host has asserted her right under the Copyright, Design and Patents Act 1988 to be identified as the author of this work.

All rights reserved. No parts of this book may be used or reproduced by any means, graphic, electronic, or mechanical, including photocopying, recording, taping or by any information storage retrieval system without the written permission of the copyright holder.

A CIP catalogue for this book is available from the British Library.

ISBN 979-8-857-602-12-6 (pbk)

Cover design and typesetting by Arch Publishing Services

www.archpub.net

Printed and bound in Great Britain

Contents

PART TWO

PART THREE

For Emily Hope and Eowyn Rose, the future is yours.

Preface

2024 will see the 30th anniversary of the ordination of women to the priesthood into the Church of England. I was one of those women. This book is my reflection on my part in that historic date and the years that followed.

My hope in telling my story, is that it might be of help to others. I wanted to be open about my experiences, so I have included a description of an extended period of psychotherapy which formed an important part of my growth and healing.

It is a mystery to me how the girl who left grammar school aged 16, barely scraping four GCE O levels in English literature, English language, domestic science and history, should have become 'one of the first'.

It has been a journey without maps, but maybe not without a divine plan.

Love makes both the lover and the beloved more truly human.
Tom Wright, *John for Everyone* (p. 74)

Oh, the comfort, the inexpressible comfort of feeling safe with a person; having neither to weigh thoughts nor measure words, but to put them all out, just as they are, chaff and grain together, knowing that a faithful hand will take and sift them, keep what is worth keeping, and then, with a breath of kindness, blow the rest away.
Dinah Maria (Mulock) Craik, *A Life for a Life*, 1859

Introduction

PURPLE INTO GOLD

I love the colour purple. I didn't know until relatively recently that purple suited me. A friend who was starting a new business wanted to try out her new skills of colour analysis, so she asked me to be a guinea pig. As the many coloured cloths wafted next to my skin, my eyes were opened. A palette of soft pinks, blues and purple brought my face alive. It was then that I fell in love with purple.

Purple is a deeply symbolic colour in the Christian Church, it is on display in the reflective seasons of Lent and Advent, it is the colour of preparation, repentance and mourning. By contrast, it is also an imperial colour. In Roman times only emperors could wear purple. Today it is worn by many Bishops in the Church of England. It is also worn by priests as they conduct funerals, marking them as occasions for sadness and loss.

Purple is never the end of the story; it leads into gold. The purple of Advent leads us to the high feast of Christmas Gold.

Lent takes us to the even more glorious feast of Easter. Gold is the destination, the celebration and the purpose; purple leads us there. There is no gold without purple. I love them both.

This is the journey of purple into gold, my journey of healing and hope.

Part One

Chapter One

SWITZERLAND

My journey towards being one of the first women priests began when I worked as an au pair in Lausanne, Switzerland. Of course, I didn't know that then. In the autumn of 1973, I left my home for Lausanne to begin my new adventure. Most au pairs are recruited for the task of childcare. Mercifully, no child was entrusted to my care at the raw age of eighteen! Instead, my job involved caring for six dogs and one old lady. It was popular to be an au pair in the 1970s.

One of my daily tasks was to keep the apartment looking as though it was not lived in. For this job, spring cleaning was never just seasonal. I was told this was the Swiss way, and I was lucky because the Swiss Germans were reputed to be even more fastidious. To be fair, it wasn't just homes that were kept in immaculate condition; the buses, trains and streets were litter free. This became apparent to me when, in a moment of absent mindedness while onboard a bus, I emptied my coat

3

pockets of spent tickets onto the floor. This caused a collective glare from the other passengers. So I swiftly picked them up.

Each day as an au pair started with the coffee machine, waiting to be loaded with freshly ground coffee beans, resulting in a rich aroma accompanied the steady percolating liquid. Next to attend to, was the dishwasher. As a working-class girl from the black country, both gadgets were new to me. Then, the dogs had to be taken out for a walk. Once I was back in the apartment, the daily round of housekeeping and laundry began. The routine was dreary and exhausting, but it was made just a little better by a balcony which looked out onto the beautiful Lac Leman. Beyond that, weas the majesty of the mountains across the lake in Evian, France.

The daily grind was all worthwhile, for the nightlife of Lausanne gave me the opportunity to learn French.

I had arrived in Lausanne in the pursuit of a dream of freedom and adventure and I had bought a one-way air ticket. With me in the city, were young adults from all over the world, some were students, and many were like me, au pair girls. Lausanne was a melting pot of nationalities and here I had my first encounter with Scandinavians, Americans, Italians and even a few Swiss!

This way of life was all so different, even the music was new to me. Today, many years later, when I hear the song 'Forever and ever' by Demis Roussos, I am transported back to a nightclub called, ironically, Funny Hell. I loved him. I had never heard of him back home, but in Europe, he was one of the biggest stars.

Another place we gathered, those of us a long way from home, was a British style pub called Pickwicks. I loved it there too. It was a little pocket of home; somewhere to meet people and make friends. Carole, another au pair, was a couple of years older than me and she had been in Lausanne for nearly a year. We became firm friends, and she helped me find my feet in this new and exciting adventure.

Despite a grammar school education, at the start of my time as an au pair my knowledge of French was barely basic. When I arrived at Geneva airport, even to utter the word *merci* to the taxi driver, left me tongue-tied. Nonetheless, my experience is testimony to the value of the immersion method of language learning as within three months I had a competent level of French. By that point I could shop confidently at the local boucherie, boulangerie and candlestick maker. Lausanne was a delightful place to learn French, as the local Vaudois accent, with its musicality and slower pace, makes it easier to hear.

This international city was home to major sporting events, it had a rich cultural life and an international university. However, to me it was my local town and after a short while living there, I could move around it with an ease, negotiating the always-on-time public transport system. The buses in Lausanne were a model of Swiss punctuality and efficiency. It was futile to arrive at a bus stop half a minute late with the hope that the bus might be running a little late. It never was.

Waiting for a bus in Lausanne was an eye-opener. I experienced the Swiss as conservative and introverted by temperament, but when the bus arrived, their shadow side emerged as they dashed to board it. Whatever else may be said about the British, we know how to queue. The Swiss, it seemed, did not.

Switzerland is known for its mountains, but even the towns and cities are hilly and Lausanne being no exception. I had one day off a week, and on this day I could usually be found teetering along one of the most popular streets in my platform heeled boots. It was steep. Lausanne carried with it the heady aroma of ground coffee percolating the air and though I am not a coffee drinker, this smell was intoxicating. Another favourite place of mine to visit was Mario's Pizza Parlour. Mario's was popular, it had a rustic air, with white painted walls and wooden tables and chairs. The walls were regularly covered with graffiti, renewed every time the walls were repainted; it was a multi-lingual and humorous place to be. At Mario's, pizzas were made on the premises, stretched, and spun and then cooked in the clay ovens. These were the days before the ubiquity of pizza restaurants. It was here that I had my first taste of a margarita pizza, the like of which has never since tasted as good. Many a Saturday evening was spent at Mario's eating pizza and drinking red wine.

Life as an au pair required attendance at language school three afternoons a week. A student visa was the way most families recruited their au pairs. This might be considered modern day-slavery now as an au pair on a student visa was poorly paid and bonded to the family who hired you. If you left their employ, the only choice you had was to live on the charity of others or return home.

It was at language school that I befriended a young Californian woman, who, like me, was working for a family. Barbara was a warm companion and, as it turned out, also like me, she was a cradle Catholic. Unlike me, she was still attending church and her religious practice was important to her. I was amazed to learn this. I had been a very religious child, catching a bus by myself every Sunday morning to attend mass, but I had long since abandoned this when I hit adolescence.

Going to church and attending a Roman Catholic primary school had been important to me as a child, it had been one of the few stable things about my young life. But, like many teenagers, I had concluded the church was either for the very young and innocent or for the very old and lonely, and no help to me. One reason for this, was my struggle with the obligation to attend confession regularly to be good enough to go to church. It is one thing to go to confession when your sins fall into the category of fighting with brothers and sisters. 'I fought with my brothers and sisters' was a regular lament of mine, and it is quite easy to admit to those 'sins'. When life becomes a murkier, it is a little different. Even missing Sunday mass was classed as a mortal sin, and I'd missed too many of those to count.

So I soon concluded that there was no way I was going to rock up to some random, celibate priest and make my confession. After that, I believed my churchgoing days were over. And yet, at times during those years, I would regret this decision. There were times during my teenage years when I would think to myself, 'If only I hadn't stopped going to church, maybe I wouldn't be in the mess I am now.' But I didn't know how to start again. I felt as though my sins had piled up like unpaid debts, and my spiritual bank was empty.

Lausanne was the opportunity I was looking for to start a new chapter. I could leave behind the baggage of my life and begin again. Freedom beckoned and there was no better place to reinvent myself than in a foreign country.

I was grateful for Barbara's friendship, we hung out together at language school and every week she invited me to join her at the English-speaking Catholic church in Lausanne. The problem being it was on a Sunday.

Saturday nights were precious. Sunday was the one morning I didn't have to get up early to walk the dogs. So, getting up to go to church had little appeal and for a few weeks I declined.

However, the desire for friendship and a latent desire to please, meant that one Sunday I gave in and went along to church with Barbara. The congregation met in the basement of a modern apartment block in a suburb of Lausanne.

To my absolute horror, I burst into tears as soon as the service started, and I continued to weep all through mass. I was sobbing among strangers as the familiar words of the liturgy washed around me. Why was I crying, what moved me so immediately to tears? It was as though I had found something that I didn't even realise I had lost.

The service ended, a lovely parish priest offered me warmth, welcome and inclusion. I don't remember his name, but I do remember his grace and humanity. When I had attended church as a child, the mass had been still said in Latin; the priests performed the eucharistic rite, and all that was expected of the congregation was to turn up and watch. This new experience of churchgoing was entirely different. Lay people offered prayers and read the day's Bible readings, and I had an epiphanic moment. I thought, 'Of course, church was always supposed to be for the people who showed up – it was never supposed to be a spectator sport!'

How had the Church got that so wrong? How does it still get it so wrong? A church was never intended to function like a cosy social club, affording comfort to its existing membership whilst at the same time, suspicious of anyone who doesn't look familiar.

The realisation I had on that day has never left me. It is an insight I have tried to hold onto throughout my ministry. When a church gathers for worship, it is supposed to be welcoming and inclusive, especially when someone has taken the huge, scary decision to enter a church for the first time.

At that moment, the embers of Christian faith were stirred

in me again. I had found my way back and I didn't want to get lost again. Through this, other friendships were formed within a lively Christian group. Coinciding with my return to church life, the evangelist Billy Graham visited Lausanne. Preparations for the Lausanne Congress were underway, and he was to be the main attraction.

It was March 1974 and Billy Graham was the guest speaker to a smaller gathering of English and French speaking women. He was a warm and charismatic speaker and with a line-by-line translation from English to French, he told the story of the 23rd Psalm. The evangelist concluded, saying if anyone wanted to begin a personal relationship with God, through Jesus Christ, they should raise their hand. This was an intimate gathering, unlike the usual stadium arenas where he would invite people to come forward. Here with heads bowed, we were invited to raise a hand. I was alarmed, and I'll be honest, I hesitated. Surely now I was ok, I had started going to church again, what more did I need to do? A few moments passed before I made my first faltering steps into an adult Christian faith. I gave my life to God and asked him to be in charge from now on.

Walking home from the centre of Lausanne to the village where I lived, fog descended obscuring the surrounding mountains. But on this March afternoon there was a new clarity within me. A new hope was born. In the years since then, I have often pondered the story of The Prodigal Son, a story found in the gospel of Luke. It is a parable telling the story of a young man who felt the need to get as far away from home as he could. He lived the high life and spent all his money on wine, women, and song. Once he had run out of money, he was reduced to feeding pigs to make a living, so hungry himself, that he considered eating their food. Eventually he came to his senses and began the long journey home. That's what it felt like for me. I felt as if I had come to my senses and was at the start of a journey home. Not that I planned or even wanted to return to the home I had left, some years before, it felt more like a homecoming of the soul.

For many years I described this experience as 'the day I became a Christian' or being 'born again' as though it all began on that March day in Lausanne. I considered my childhood devotions as irrelevant. I'm not sure when I began to change my mind about that, but at some point I began to remember spiritual experiences from my primary school days.

St. Mary and All Angels, Roman Catholic Primary School, fed us on a regular diet of religious education as it was called then. In one lesson I recall now, we learned a new version of the 23rd Psalm. As I sang the lyrics, 'his goodness shall follow me always, to the end of my days', I had a profound sense of the truth of those words for me. I was nine years old. Maybe the Almighty had been on the case for much longer than I since gave credit for.

On that March day, I fell in love with Jesus, and my new Christian faith was nurtured by the friends I had recently made and the welcome of the church I attended. So, it was a sad day when my time in Switzerland was over, and like young adults everywhere, even today, when there is nowhere else to go, and no money left, it becomes time to go home. This time I was not leaving on a jet plane, but in a berth on a lengthy cross Europe train.

At midnight one July evening in 1974, as the train pulled out of Lausanne station, I said goodbye to my Lausanne adventure with a hope that I might return one day. It was a different person who returned to the UK to the one who had left a year before.

Chapter Two

HOMECOMING

The return home was a huge step for me because, in my head I had left home some while before my departure for Switzerland. Home for me was a place I had always planned to leave at the earliest opportunity. My early career choice of hotel receptionist was due in large part because, thanks to odd shift patterns, accommodation was provided for hotel employees. This return was not to a welcome of robe, ring and fatted calf, in the manner of a prodigal daughter, but to a household already too small for its existing residents: mother, father, two sisters and one brother. Two older brothers were long gone from home, though one would later return with a girlfriend and young son in tow. It was not a homecoming to the bosom of a happy family.

Why did I return? One reason was lack of money and opportunity to stay in Switzerland. With my new-found Christian faith, I didn't want to resume the precarious life of hotel work; I somehow felt it wouldn't be good for me. I also had a new sense of needing to be led into God's plan for my life, so I tried to settle back into the dysfunction of my family with a belief that I could change things for the better. Perhaps I did change some things for some of my family. My two sisters and brother became curious about the Christian faith, they could see that I was different. I tried to cultivate a better relationship with my parents; I strove to understand why my father was the way he was. I prayed regularly for him; by now he was quite disabled. I prayed that he would improve both in health and temper. Surely my responsibility now was to forgive. I asked myself: isn't forgiveness the hallmark of a true Christian? It would be many years before I really began to see him for the damaged and damaging person he was. Somehow, I brought to my return home an expectation that I could rescue my family. After all, hadn't I been rescued through becoming a Christian? Didn't I owe it to them? I didn't know it then, but I didn't owe them anything. It felt as though, I had escaped once, but now I was trapped again.

So there I was, home again, the place where I had lived since the age of six, left at the age of seventeen, to return aged twenty. I knew it was important to find a church, a place where I could grow in my new-found faith, a place to belong. However, I didn't anticipate staying around for long. My plan, or rather my hope, was that there would be a calling of some kind to missionary work so I could share my new-found faith. In my fantasy moments, I imagined that one day I might become another Billy Graham!

But first, the task was to find a local church. I went back to the Roman Catholic church I attended as a child, but quickly realised this would not provide the experience I looked for. What I wanted was a church like the one in Lausanne. I realise now how naïve that sounds. I made a few enquiries about where I might find a 'lively' church, only to discover that very near to my parents' home was a new church, a daughter church of the older parish church. I had already visited the parish church to introduce myself.

The first time I made my way to the new daughter church, a voice nagged on my shoulder, it whispered, 'Who do you think you are going to church like a normal person?' I pressed on and found my way to a building that could just as easily have been a community centre located at the heart of a new housing estate. There was not a pew in sight. I joined the congregation, and soon after the service I met my first Church of England vicar, Malcolm. He had already heard about a young woman newly returned from a Francophone country; word had got out about me, as it does when someone new turns up on the churches radar. Malcolm approached and started speaking in French! He was a French graduate and keen to converse, so, for several minutes we chatted away in French. I hadn't seen that coming!

Meeting Malcolm was the best introduction to the Church of England I could have had, and to this day I am grateful for his courage and warmth as he welcomed me into his fold. My faith was nurtured, I was encouraged to take part in his church's life and he gave me the opportunity to spread my wings and develop my gifts. Malcolm saw in me a gift for communication. And one Easter Sunday, he asked me to speak about what this feast meant to me. I was thrilled, there was so much I wanted to share about my new faith, and without any trepidation, I went for it! Afterwards, Malcolm came alongside me, and with a quiet voice said, 'When the time is right, you should consider training to be a lay preacher.' I did not realise how radical this was, women had only recently been allowed to be lay preachers and I was only twenty-one!

The right time came a couple of years later. By this time, I had met and married my husband Ian, and we were living in our own home. I can't remember now exactly how I went from being encouraged to consider life as a preacher to being one of a group of men and women who began training together. Malcolm had planted the seeds in my mind, and when the chance came to be part of a new course that was starting, I was up for it. As a group we were fortunate, we had Malcolm as a tutor, he was an excellent teacher. He taught us New Testament and Old Testament, ethics and spirituality. We lapped it up, though we were less keen on the essays.

Meanwhile, in August 1979, I gave birth to our first daughter. Motherhood, though planned, interrupted study much more than I expected. and for a short while I thought of taking a year out. Malcolm counselled against this. In his wisdom, he helped me see that if I stopped, it would take a huge effort to start again, besides there may be another baby on the way by then! It was good advice, I stuck with it. At the age of twenty-seven I was licensed in Lichfield Cathedral to preach and lead worship. This was the start of a new role, I was part of the leadership in my local church, and with Malcolm's encouragement and guidance, I settled into a regular pattern of leading services and preaching.

The time came when Malcolm was ready to move to another parish, it is the way of Church of England vicars. His successor was Daniel, a talented musician who was younger than Malcolm, and someone I had met a year earlier at a music workshop. We got on famously. Daniel encouraged my musical gifts and together we developed the musical life of the congregation. We met together to plan and rehearse the music.

Working with a talented musician was the best way for me to improve musically. Even just allowing me to play the guitar alongside him felt like a huge pat on the back, and we were encouraged as we saw the church grow in numbers, in spirit and musicality.

However, our relationship wasn't all straightforward. Like all artistic people, we had our clashes. Daniel was younger than Malcolm, so less experienced and perhaps less secure. One of the early things Daniel asked me to do was let him have the text of my sermon a few days before I preached! I thought this was a bit strange at the time, I knew that as a very last-minute person I would find it quite a stretch having my sermon ready at least two days in advance. It didn't occur to me at the time that this was quite a controlling thing to do. Nevertheless, I dutifully delivered my hand-written sermon to him in advance, only to receive it back with grammar and spelling corrections. Was he checking my English ability or theological compatibility? In other words, was I 'sound' enough? I think I complied. Twice.

It was a while later that I learned that Daniel was simply repeating his own experience as a curate, as this had been required of him. Interesting how the way one has been parented, can be handed on undigested.

Those few years of working at the heart of church life were golden. I grew in confidence as a musician and worship leader. With regular use, my guitar playing skills improved, and I was fortunate to be given the opportunity to grow in creativity with the services I led. Putting together a carol service was a highlight, though trying to include everyone's favourite carol was always a challenge.

By the time my first daughter was three, I gave birth to a second. This second pregnancy was more difficult, there were problems which required a five week stay in hospital leading to a Caesarean section. Life became more challenging with a three-year-old, a baby and a husband who worked in a demanding job. Ian was as supportive as he could be when not in inner-city Birmingham teaching physics. Nevertheless, we kept up our high-level of commitment at church. As I think back to those times, we were foolhardy to try to do so much. Why didn't we allow ourselves more recreation time and time off to enjoy life, love, and family? Why did I battle through post-natal depression and resume church life as soon after the birth of my second daughter as I could? Could it be that I feared being forgotten if I didn't show up and play my part? I didn't know then that it was enough to be me. I felt that I had to deliver, had to perform. On the surface, it seemed like I had everything, deeper down I know now that there lurked a growing undercurrent of anxiety and unhappiness.

In a few short years both girls were at school, and at that point I began to consider my future. With a résumé which included, hotel, au pair and clerical work, my options were limited. I had left grammar school at sixteen with four O levels, I would have to return to education if I wanted a profession. But to do what? I considered training to be a teacher but quickly realised that though I loved my own, I was not keen enough on anyone else's children to want to spend my working life with them!

So I pondered if there a way to work for the church. I began to wonder if there was any way to grow my ministry. I was well loved at my local church and almost anything I did was appreciated, but it had become comfortable recently, the challenge had diminished, and I had become restless. Over the years I have learned that life begins at the edge of your comfort zone, so I decided to talk it over with the vicar, Daniel.

Around this time, we had a new kitchen fitted in our four-bedroomed house. Like many of our friends, we had a large mortgage, leaving just enough spare cash to do a much-needed remodel of the kitchen. Little did I know how significant that kitchen would be in my enquiry about ordination.

I asked to meet with Daniel. I wanted to share my ideas about my future, ask his opinion, seek his counsel. The conversation started like this:

'Daniel, I've been wondering about what to do next with my life. I preach and lead worship regularly, and I've been thinking might God be calling me into ministry, to become a deaconess?'

(These were the days long before women were ordained priest, they were not yet even deacons. A deaconess was usually a single woman, and although occasionally she might be engaged in a full-time paid position, she was still not a member of the clergy. This didn't bother me, the stirring I felt was towards a more formal role of church leadership, I had no design at this stage to be a priest.)

Without a moment's hesitation, Daniel replied:

'Oh, I think God wants you to enjoy your new kitchen a little longer.'

Yes. Of course, that's what God wanted. And dear reader, I took it. I heard those words from this man who I admired, who had inspired and encouraged me musically. If it stirred anger in me then, I don't remember. It does now.

Daniel was compromised. Whilst Malcolm before him had no issue with women in leadership, he simply looked on gifting rather than gender, Daniel, who was more conservative theologically, was not at all sure whether women really should be leaders in the Church. He further compounded the insult with this:

'But I could see Ian doing it.'

These were my first hints that being a woman in the Church's ministry and having a leadership role would make a difference to the path my life would take. I was yet to discover the capacity a patriarchal institution had for being utterly patronising and how that would impact me.

Chapter Three

BERYL'S GIRLS

Fortunately for me, there was another authority figure, besides Daniel, I could appeal to. This was Beryl, the head deaconess of our diocese. After my discussion with Daniel, I went along to meet her. She opened the door to me and out came the word 'sherry!' It confirmed all my worst fears about Church of England clergy, that they are all a bunch of out-of-touch, alcohol drinking, middle-aged has-beens! A somewhat arrogant statement, I can see now. In fact, Beryl had not been offering me a sherry, she was calling her dog to attention.

Our conversation that day was inconclusive, and I left wondering where I should go next. Beryl suggested I return to see her later if I wanted to pursue a conversation about ordination. I don't remember how long I left it between visits, but I did return, and this time Beryl was more forthcoming. She told me that I had clearly moved on with my thinking since the last time we had spoken, and, yes, she was happy to support my calling towards a leadership role in the Church. That's what I thought it was, a leadership role. I didn't have any aspirations to be a priest or a deacon, in fact at that time it wouldn't have been possible to by either. But the good thing was, Beryl took me under her wing. I no longer had to consider whether God wanted me to appreciate my new kitchen. I was one of Beryl's girls, much to the annoyance of Daniel.

Life moved on very quickly after becoming one of 'Beryl's girls'. An interview with the Bishop was arranged, and after a short conversation with him I was sent to a selection conference. In those days, the selection conferences involved a three-day residency at a retreat centre with other vicar hopefuls. There was also a Bishops' Advisory Panel, comprising of a conference secretary, an academic, a lay person and another senior member of the clergy. The fantasy I had was that these people were out to get me.

The church I belonged to had a deep suspicion of the wider Church as an institution, we even suspected that a lot of them were simply not Christians. As a result, I knew I had to put on a 'good show' and choose my words carefully. I was on high alert. It didn't help that the day I left for the selection conference I came down with a bout of thrush, an unpleasant ailment suffered mainly by women. I had never suffered from it before, so added to my anxiety was an uncomfortable itch that I was too embarrassed to admit.

The selection conference involved a series of interviews plus three group exercises where I was observed to see how I handled group discussions. It was draining; I was a long way from home and anxious. There was a drive to perform well whilst at the same time remain truthful. Eventually, it was over, and I returned home, to nervously await the outcome. Was I good enough? Did I qualify? These were questions buried deep in my psyche, it would be years before I recognised these were some of the drivers of my vocation.

I was due to start the course in a few days, but that would only be possible if I had been recommended for training. Within the week, head deaconess Beryl, phoned me to say I had indeed been recommended. I was ecstatic. I was being launched from my local church. Now I would get to swim in a bigger pond, now I would be one of the grown-ups. My rose-tinted glasses were firmly in place.

Training for ordination involved a three-year, part-time course at theological college. One evening a week I drove to Queen's College, Birmingham, and one weekend a month I was in residence. The part-time course was the only option for me because I still had to juggle life as a mother of two young children with a husband who was working full-time. I would have preferred to train full-time, and although Ian was fully supportive, that was just not possible. As a school leaver aged 16, I never had had the chance of higher education, and I was hungry to be immersed in learning. However, I wasn't really prepared for the experience of theological college. Having been granted my dream of a bigger pool in which to swim, I soon felt like a minnow swimming among sharks. The diverse opinions I encountered at college unsettled me. This was an ecumenical college, drawing students from different denominations and wildly differing theological positions. It felt as though all my negative suspicions about the Church of England were justified. This was 1987, and I had landed in a maelstrom of debate about whether women could be ordained, could re-marry as divorcees, and what was to be done about homosexuality.

The theological tribe I belonged to was evangelical and charismatic, with it came a strong emphasis on the authority of the Bible, a personal relationship with Jesus and an openness to the work of the Holy Spirit. We were clear about beliefs that were 'sound' and those that weren't. I felt that I was surrounded by people training for ordination who had some very dodgy beliefs and practices. Unfortunately, I became a self-appointed defender of the faith, as I saw it, and, in many respects, a difficult student as I constantly contested what I was being taught. It was years before I understood this defensiveness was as much to do with my lack of confidence about learning as it was about feeling vulnerable in this unfamiliar context. I had not yet grasped that it was ok for people to hold different opinions to me and that it did not invalidate my experience.

Strangely, I saw this play out many years later at art school, when a visiting lecturer was introducing the various 20th-century art movements. One of the students kept interrupting, complaining that she didn't understand the terms he was using. I found this so frustrating and challenged her when she took over and tried to answer a question I asked of the lecturer. She exploded and promptly left the lecture, complaining that she was never allowed to speak. Her actions gave me pause for thought. I understood. She was not trying to be difficult, she wanted to learn but doubted her ability to sit with uncertainty. This student colleague reminded me of myself as a student of theology decades earlier.

The more insecure I felt, the more I felt the need to hold onto my few certainties.

Our college principal, who had been a missionary in South India, was keen to break us out of the white, Eurocentric worldview we inhabited. I was reluctant, but despite my resistance, it was enriching to experience worship from other parts of the world. Liturgies that hailed from South India, and

South America spoke of their context. I learned about apartheid in South Africa and how the Church there continued to be a hopeful presence whilst opposing the government.

At a mission to Birmingham led by Archbishop Desmond Tutu, I had the good fortune to be part of a group leading worship at the rallies he addressed. This was a turning point. Here, I heard first-hand what life was like for black South Africans, ruled by and separated from the white minority. There would have been just cause in making us feel complicit and it would have been the easiest thing in the world to send us all away feeling guilty. But there was not even a hint of condemnation. Instead, the Archbishop, with a twinkle in his eye, joyfully reminded us, that we were all loved by God in whose image we are made.

Would I have ever learned these other world views had it not been part of my formation for ministry in the Church of England? Though I thought of myself as a woman of the world, I was beginning to see that I knew very little about this world.

These were also the days before the ordination of women to the priesthood, and we had many heated discussions about the place of women in the Church. Questions were asked about whether the Bible allowed women to be in positions of leadership over men, let alone become priests alongside them. These questions raged in the wider Church with opinion divided even amongst us students.

At theological college I met feminist theologians. They lead me to reflect that my own vicar, who had always considered me to be a radical feminist, he had no clue as to what a pussy cat I was by comparison! These theologians taught me to look for the women's story in the Bible. This was often an exercise in imagination as, so often, the women were overlooked or simply forgotten. Later in life I was to learn that the art world had traditionally faced a similar problem, women artists have simply been excluded from art history. One such artist is Artemesia Gentileschi, a highly successful painter from the same era as Caravaggio, who only recently has been rediscovered and celebrated.

Similarly, in Christian history, Mary Magdalene, a follower of Jesus, remained unacknowledged as 'the apostle to the apostles', and the first to give testimony to the resurrection of Jesus.

One thing that confounded me during my time at college was that the students who I judged to be rather woolly in what they believed, seemed to have a greater confidence than I that they were loved by God. How did that equate?

One day when a lecturer quoted these words from the gospel, 'Lord, I believe, help my unbelief' describing them as a healthy approach in prayer, I was shocked. Surely, we should be certain of our beliefs. To me, this was one more example of woolly Christianity.

Today, three decades later, I know the reality of that prayer.

Faith is not about being sure of everything, it is more a willingness to trust. The words were first spoken by a man who was asking Jesus to heal his son. He wanted to believe that Jesus could heal him, at the same time, he was also aware of his own uncertainty.

For me, the prayer had a reality. There have been times over the years when I have seriously wondered what the Divine was up to! For example, one Christmas Eve I received news that a friend of my daughter's had died unexpectedly. Aside from the tragedy for the family, it was the least convenient time for me, and I told God as much as I made my way to visit his parents. I had already conducted several Christmas services and Midnight Mass was still to come, I felt I had nothing to offer. And I wasn't sure God had anything to offer. Not knowing what I would face, all I could do was trust that God would heed the hurried words of my prayers. How he would answer them, I knew not. There seemed little at Theological College that prepared me for times like this.

The trouble with the teaching at college was that it all seemed so experimental. What I wanted was more systematic teaching about the Old and New Testament; I felt that we were getting an 'eat as much as you like' buffet made up of appetisers. It was tasty but ultimately unsatisfying. It left me wanting a main meal of biblical learning that would sustain me in the days and years of parish ministry that lay ahead. It put me in mind of the introduction of comprehensive schools in the 1960s; I recall apocryphal rumours of young people leaving school at the age of 16 having had a rich experience of education, learning Italian and other exotic subjects, but with little grasp of the three Rs. That is how my theological education and ministry formation felt. I didn't feel adequately equipped for life as a parish priest.

Ian became used to me arriving home after college on a Tuesday evening ranting about how the evening had gone. In my classes I was looking for confirmation of what I believed, but when I was being asked to consider alternative viewpoints, it felt like a personal rejection. I was trying to change the world around me, not realising that I only had the power to change myself. I had not yet learned the prayer known as the Serenity Prayer.

God, grant me the serenity to accept the things I cannot change, the courage to change the things I can, and the wisdom to know the difference.

And though I had a deep sense of being called by God to a wider role of preaching and leading worship, I had doubts about whether there would really be a place for me at the end of all this.

Nevertheless, there were some delights among this buffet. Once a year, the student body became residential so that we could have a deeper period of formation. One year, we were fortunate to be joined by two members of the Iona Community. The Iona Community, and its partner, The Wild Goose Worship, group, value and promote the Celtic origins of Christianity. A leading light of this community is John Bell. John has a great gift for teaching and writing prayers and songs for use in worship. Today he has a worldwide reputation, but in the late 1980s he was just getting going.

John had an amazing impact on our community. As a student body we were well used to being divided into different camps, both theologically, and in style of worship. John Bell brought us all together. Somehow, he offered us a third way, something that we could all buy into. John was someone we all loved, and the resources he brought to us have stayed with me throughout my ministry.

Eventually, it was time to leave, and to move onto what it had all been for. I was glad to leave, vowing I would never return. But, as they say, never say never, and a few years later I did return to upgrade my learning and qualification to a BA in Applied Theological Studies.

Chapter Four

On this day, Coventry cathedral was full, among the congregation were friends, family and strangers from my new church that I hoped would also become friends. Though the famous cathedral, built among the remains of a World War II bombing, was still unfamiliar to me. There was a sense of hushed anticipation as those of us to be ordained made our way into the cathedral. Ordinations are occasions of great pomp and ceremony, with bishops in their full regalia, and cathedral clergy looking equally important in theirs. The music was majestic with the cathedral choir and organ on duty. All of it heightened the solemnity and my anxiety. It felt surreal.

I was relieved to see my husband, Ian, with our two daughters, who were now eight and eleven years old. I took my place alongside them. The pre-ordination retreat meant that I hadn't seen them for several days, and now here we were, me, fully clad in my deacon's robe, and they, in their Sunday best.

Days spent at the retreat centre had left me feeling lonely, isolated, as I tried, in my mind, to minimise the step I was about to take. I hadn't slept well. I didn't know any of the other candidates for ordination because I was a newcomer to this diocese. My own sending diocese, Lichfield, were struggling to find positions for all of its new deacons, especially as a good number of us were women. Many of the all-male clergy still hadn't got their heads around the fact they would soon have ordained women among them which made them reluctant to consider us as potential colleagues. Added to that, few of the male clergy had never even worked with a woman as a colleague, even fewer had had one as a boss.

Fortunately, I was offered a curacy in Coventry, which is how I found myself on this day wearing a deacon's robe, which is a long-sleeved, black, dress-like garment with a white cotton surplice over the top. I was used to robes like this as a preacher. What was new was the red stole that would be worn across the body at a key moment in the service. It is not unlike the kind of sash a Miss World contestant would wear. Now, I wonder if anyone else has made that connection?

This sash symbolises the time Jesus washed his disciples' feet and dried them with the towel he had wrapped around him. It symbolises the role of a servant, and at one level I knew this, but did I really understand its significance?

Many more of my friends and family joined me on that day; they followed me to a reception at my new church. It felt bittersweet to finally begin this new chapter for which I had prepared, at the same time as saying farewell to friends who had supported me. They were not just church friends, they were family friends, people I had laughed and cried with, women who had shared in the experiences of childbirth and parenting. And here I was, about to move to an area I didn't know and to a community of strangers. Would they accept me? Would they love me? What was I doing? Unacknowledged anxiety grew in my soul, and in a few desperate moments I found a private space and prayed. But I couldn't pray, the words would not come. Thank God for prayer memory that enabled me to recite the Lord's Prayer.

Life as an ordained minister had begun.

The trouble was, I still lived forty miles away, thanks to a stubborn Diocesan Secretary who had resisted buying a house for us. Tied housing is the norm for most ordained clergy. It sounds great having a house to go with your job, but when you have lived in your own home for several years, it feels quite a sacrifice to suddenly lose control of your own housing. So, for nearly three months, I had a round trip commute of eighty miles for midweek church meetings and Sunday services. It was not a good start.

From the highs of the ordination day, as my new life started, I fell into a kind of no-man's land. I didn't belong where we were still living anymore but was a stranger to the church I was working for. Our daughters were due to start new schools and the start of term was approaching.

Finally, we had a moving date; a four-bedroomed, semi-detached house was bought for us to move into. But there was another problem. I arrived home one evening, after another eighty-mile round trip, a week before our moving date, to find that my husband was ill. It was his birthday and I had already felt guilty about leaving him. As the night went on Ian became worse until eventually I called a doctor who decided to send him to hospital. I was in a daze, what was happening? We were due to move house in a few days' time, we still had to pack. It turned out Ian had appendicitis, and I couldn't see how we would be ready to move house with him being unwell. Thankfully friends came to help, and we moved house, leaving our family home behind. It was too late to change my mind.

A new job, house, and new schools do not make life easy for a new curate. Somehow, we managed it, but the added stress took its toll, and I was in the midst of it all trying to manage everyone's new life. I don't think I allowed myself, or was allowed by the vicar, to give enough attention to the mental strain of this.

The church where I served as curate had three centres. There was the main parish church and two satellite congregations. One of the satellite congregations met in a village hall, and the other met in a local school. I was the main clergy contact at the church that met in the school. This was a lively bunch of people who turned up every Sunday to turn the school hall into a church sanctuary. I realised later, that I was given far too much responsibility for my first post, I was literally left to it. Though not quite. There was at least one male lay leader who was keen to report back to the vicar. Every Sunday, I would drive to the school and sit in the car park to brace myself before going inside to the bustle of setting up and preparation for the service. I felt inadequate, not good enough. But I didn't recognise these anxieties for what they were. Neither did I feel able to tell anyone how I felt; I had to prove I was capable. I felt afraid of not being good enough, afraid of criticism, afraid of disapproval. As women we had worked hard to earn our place at the table, it wouldn't be good to be seen as not coping and admit that I was struggling. I had a fear that this would confirm the suspicions that we women were not up to it. This church community was full of professional people, and compared to them, I keenly felt my lack of education and professional background.

I had already been paraded round some of the key lay

people during the interview process. When one woman asked what I read at university, I had to admit that I hadn't been to university. Her husband was a university lecturer. It didn't help either that the congregation I was attached to didn't really want an ordained person around; it seemed to me, they were quite happy sorting themselves out. The expression 'all chiefs and no Indians' came to mind, except that I felt like I was the only Indian!

It felt like I was the new curate in a church that didn't really know what to do with a curate. The trouble was at theological college, I, along with my student colleagues, was encouraged to think creatively. The culture in training was to challenge and question long held beliefs. Did God always have to be male, could she be a mother figure? Was Jesus really a blue-eyed, long-haired white man? No, of course not. But the parish wasn't ready for such discussions, and I wasn't ready for what was required of me.

What was required of me was to fit in: keep my head down, learn what I needed to learn and move on. I know now that this was not going to be my long-term post. Unfortunately, I didn't have the wisdom then to see this, and it made for an uncomfortable relationship with the vicar.

I had such high hopes of ordained life, but it felt like being forced into a mould that was not of my choosing. I was looking for encouragement, affirmation and the chance to grow in the gifts that I believed I had. I didn't get that. I risked asking for affirmation during one tense staff meeting. I asked, 'Don't you think I have any gifting for this role?' A reluctant reply came, 'you have some gifts.' Ian revealed to me years later that the vicar had spoken to him privately and said it would be better if I left the ministry and returned home.

Years later, in therapy, I gained a better understanding of

the situation I was in, I had been looking for approval from an authority figure. My early childhood was devoid of encouragement and approval and so I was seeking it in adulthood. Already, I had experienced being a grammar school failure, and as a result, I had little self-esteem. Through the encouragement of my sending church, I had begun to flourish, yet the inner child still craved the approval and recognition denied as an infant.

I began to wonder if I was experiencing depression and eventually, I went to my local GP, who also thought I might be depressed and prescribed a course of anti-depressants. There was little explanation of why I might be depressed or even what depression was. I was just grateful to receive the pills that I was assured would help. I didn't make the connection between how I felt and the stress of my ministry. Though waking every night with an attack of asthma, which left me reaching for my inhaler, should have told me that this was not normal. I didn't recognise that I was simply unhappy.

I could have asked to be placed in another parish, but my family had already had one upheaval and I didn't want to inflict another upon them. My daughters were at local schools, we had new friends locally and at church, I didn't want to let them down. And, though I felt unsupported by the church leaders, there were some fantastic people around who appreciated what I was bringing, and despite the difficulties I experienced, some lifelong friendships were formed.

Yes, I could have asked to move but I believed things could improve. Experience has taught me that it is hard to leave a situation that is difficult. There is always an inner driver telling you that you can make it work, and that the situation can be rescued if only you try a little harder. It is a mindset that has deep psychological roots; it also explains why some people become trapped in toxic situations.

After three years, it was time to move on. Senior staff in the diocese recognised that this had not been the best start for me, and they were keen to find another post where my training could continue. This was also the time before women were ordained as priests, so my options were limited.

Allow me to introduce, the Reverend Canon A. Gardener.

Chapter Five

ONE OF THE FIRST

Tony Gardener was someone who could be described as a wise old bird. He had trained countless curates, and there would be more to come after me. The Bishop had asked him about taking me on, and Tony invited me over to the midweek communion service. It was 28th October, the feast of St. Jude the apostle, often known as the patron saint of hopeless causes. The timing was accidental.

I was offered the position of associate minister; it was still a training post, but at least it was one that recognised I had received some initial formation. Still, I'm sure the church always saw me as the 'new curate'.

Tony was a kind and generous man, he loved his flock, and they loved him, but he was no push over. The church reflected his kindness, and they were wonderfully kind to me. This was a place to heal some of my brokenness. Tony was someone to whom the term 'politically correct' would never apply. The words he used to introduce me to the congregation were:

'You'll have noticed its better looking at the front of the church than it usually is, this is Charmaine.'

Early on Tony told me two things:

The first: 'I like to get my colleagues onto a good living.' Already he was preparing me for what lay ahead, he would be on the lookout for the right job for me.

The second: 'You make your own work; I always give my colleagues enough rope to hang themselves!'

This was a new experience for me, here was someone who trusted me. More wisdom came when he said:

'People think that having a curate is cheap labour, it's not, it's expensive labour preparing them for wider ministry.' He was as good as his word.

Tony was a man of great faith, a faith that had been severely tested by the illness of his much-loved daughter who had lost her sight through diabetes. Rachel had been a long-awaited child, and it was cruel that she was struck down at such a young age. But he never lost his faith in Jesus, and it was as if his own broken heart made it all the larger for others.

In the winter of 1993 we moved into a tiny three-bedroomed, semi-detached house. It was a struggle, one room had to be fitted with a cabin bed so that there was enough room for oldest daughter to have somewhere to store clothing as well as sleep. I resented living in such cramped conditions. Later, I was able to persuade Tony to have a small extension put on the house so that we could have a downstairs loo and utility room. There was a rumour that Tony was always more amendable to me than he had been to my predecessors, because I was a woman. I think that's probably true. With me, he adopted an almost fatherly attitude, which I was grateful for. A kind father figure had always been absent from my life.

Ian and I were loved in that church. I was loved and my

ministry was welcomed and affirmed by Tony and his congregation. It was fitting then that the ordination of women to the priesthood happened during my time at this church. The congregation, which had launched many curates into church life, deserved to be part of this historic moment.

On 23rd April 1994, Coventry Cathedral was full again.

Barely four years had passed, and I was now one of thirty, riding the wave of this new tide of women being fully admitted into the priesthood. There would be some time and many more arguments yet before women were admitted to the office of Bishop. Even on this day, one brave man was permitted to stand and formally put his objections to the presiding Bishop. It had been expected and included as part of the procedure. The Church of England can tolerate most things if they are agreed in advance and included in a liturgy. The objection was heard and acknowledged by the bishop but declined, this evoked spontaneous applause from the congregation. So, along with many other women in cathedrals up and down the land, this historic event made its mark, I was ordained priest. One of the first.

Of course, we were all the first, all the women priests were the first. Some had waited many years for this day hardly daring to hope that it would ever happen, many of the women were already in their retirement years. At the age of thirty-nine, I was one of the youngest. It still surprises me now how often I am greeted with the delighted query: 'Oh, were you one of the first?'

The terror of the July day when I was ordained deacon, had been overcome with experience, the passage of time, and grace, By the momentous day of 23rd April 1994, I had settled into being a minister in the Church of England. For me the journey towards priesthood had been a relatively short one, but whether a short or long wait, here we all were in our black cassocks, white surplices and red stoles that had now changed from being a Miss World type sash to a long scarf. A deacon's stole became a priest's stole.

Some of the sisterhood had gone to town on their new vestments for this occasion. One rather glamourous woman had gone for haute couture. She was tall, slim and elegant. It was my misfortune to be positioned in front of her as we processed into the cathedral. I felt anything but tall and slim, even my hair was having a bad day! This was still the era of curly perms, which didn't fare well in damp drizzly weather.

For a few days before the ordination, we had had been away on an ordination retreat. I don't remember now what the retreat leader spoke about, but there was a quiet sense of anticipation amongst us. On the morning of the ordination, we gathered at a local hotel for breakfast. Over bacon and eggs, we encouraged each other, shared stories, and contemplated the day ahead.

Unlike the hot and sunny day of my ordination as deacon, the day of my ordination as priest was a typical day of April showers and the sunshine barely made an appearance. We walked in procession, two by two, through the ruins of Coventry Cathedral and entered through the door set in the splendour of the west window. A crowd of well-wishers had braved the weather to gather and cheer us on our way. These good-hearted supporters had not been able to enter the cathedral as all the seats had been taken by invitation only. At the entrance stood a group of women holding a banner, I was nervous. Would there be protests? Was this a delegation of 'Women against Ordination'? Believe it or not, some of the most vocal opponents of women priests were, and still are, women. But no, here we were met and blessed on our way by a smiling group of Roman Catholic women whose banner read: 'Roman Catholic women for women priests'. These women were keeping faith by expressing hope, belief and longing for a day that is still unfulfilled in the Roman Catholic Church. This one simple act of solidarity moved me to tears then, and still does today as I recall it.

There was an air of anticipation in the cathedral. This long-awaited day erupted into a celebration of joy and colour. The music was sublime, the preaching superb and the sense of history being made was palpable. Friends and family turned up, again, in support.

My moment arrived. I approached the Bishop of Coventry, the Right Reverend Simon Barrington-Ward, and knelt before him. He was joined by other priest friends who shared in this act of ordination. As the Bishop laid his hands on my head, with words both simple and profound he said:

Send down the Holy Spirit upon your servant Charmaine for the office and work of a priest in your Church.

Receive this Book, as a sign of the authority which God has given you this day to preach the gospel of Christ and to minister His Holy Sacraments.

It is only as I write now, and recall those few words, that I recognise their magnitude.

More words came this time from the preacher, Dr Christina Baxter, the principal of St. John's College, Nottingham. In her sermon she reminded us of Mary Magdalene, the woman who when she met the risen Jesus in the garden, was sent to tell the other apostles of the empty tomb. They of course, typically, did not believe her and set out to see for themselves. Mary had been sent by Jesus as apostle to the apostles, somehow it had taken quite a while for the Church to catch on and affirm the place of women in the Jesus story.

For some of the women there on that day, this was the day that ended a long wait. There were tears, relief, celebrations. For me, it was overwhelming. The size and scale of it dwarfed me. This was a story in the making that was much bigger than me. It was momentous, but in a strange way it felt like it was everyone else's story, one in which I was only a small player. I've often since thought that Royal weddings might feel like this to the couple getting married, there is so much expectation hanging on the day.

Immediately after the service, there was applause, the choir sang the Hallelujah chorus, and outside the cathedral the press were waiting to interview us. I remember being engaged in a warm conversation with someone from BBC Radio Coventry & Warwickshire, but while I was talking to them, I was still asking myself, what did it all mean? Why did I still have a sense of something missing? Later that night, as I got into bed, all I could say was: 'Thank God it's all over.' But, in truth, it had only just begun.

Chapter Six

BECOMING A VICAR

My time as associate minister continued for two more years. Working alongside the rector, Tony Gardner, was illuminating. Almost everyone in the parish loved him even though he would sometimes say the most outrageous thing. Every day he would chat with the local milkman, being sure to drop into the conversation that the milkman wouldn't go to heaven if he didn't come to say his prayers at church. He was half joking.

Tony had been at the church for so long that many of the couples who came to get married had also been baptised by him as babies. He knew their parents; he'd watched them grow up and now he was preparing them for marriage. When he discovered that a couple already lived together, it was not unusual for him to take a paternal attitude towards the bride-to-be and say, 'What does your father think of that?' Again, he was half joking.

His pastoral ministry was exceptional, and he excelled with

funerals. Tony never missed the opportunity to tell people about Jesus, and that we were all destined for a better place: heaven. The first time he introduced me at a funeral happened as I waited with him at church for the hearse to arrive. He turned to the men on parade for a guard of honour, and said, 'Allow me to introduce my new colleague Charmaine, you'll want to meet her because she'll be taking your funerals next.'

I don't know if people were ever offended by his forthrightness. At a service of baptism, Tony would instruct people to be sure to put some money into the collection plate so that in turn they could be confident the church would still be in business for their next baptism. They rarely refused. There was another time when he announced the service would be quick because he felt sure that everyone would be keen to get back to the golf on television. He was a very keen golfer.

Before ordination, Tony had been a builder, he knew the importance of doing good business and staying in profit. His advice to me was to never pay a bill until it was asked for. Consequently, he was brilliant at getting people to give money to the church, and equally so in spending as little of it as possible.

But again, the time came for me to move on. Tony was as good as his word; he knew of a vacancy that was coming up in two rural parishes about ten miles away and wanted me to see it. I was asked to accompany two people to a confirmation service that was being held at the church in question. Tony wanted me to see the church and wanted the Bishop to see me. Tony would often say to me: 'It's always good to be in the way of the Bishop. Always good to be seen.'

I was not impressed with the church, the people seemed tired and discouraged and the building was not inviting. At the staff meeting the following week I gave my verdict adding that

I didn't think I would go there as vicar. 'You might not be offered it girl', was Tony's swift and sobering reply! I submitted my application.

The day for interview arrived. There were seven candidates, six men and me, and for some reason I was confident. Did I think it was a done deal? Later that day the Archdeacon phoned me to tell me that I was the successful candidate. Panic started to set in. I told him I needed to think about it overnight. That night I was in turmoil, I tossed and turned as I thought about the magnitude of what lay before me. I wanted to run, but where to? I couldn't stay where I was, and the post being offered was a good option; my children would continue at their schools, Ian could continue his job. But my anxiety was running high and part of me kept hoping that someone would ring me and tell me that they had made a mistake.

A few months later I was inducted as vicar of two rural parishes, St. Peter's Church, Kineton, and St. Margaret's Church, Combroke, with Compton Verney. The second woman vicar in the Diocese of Coventry, the first in Warwick Archdeaconry. Yes, I was to return to the people who had seemed discouraged and the place that had looked run down. I knew I would be wholly dependent on God showing up if change was to happen.

Meanwhile, I had to adapt to a rural life. I am not a country girl, up to this point I had always lived in suburbia with easy access to a chip shop, a Chinese takeaway, and a regular bus service. The week we moved house, in January 1997, was the coldest it had been for a decade. Parts of the vicarage hailed back to the 15th century and had been empty for months so with the coming and going of removal men, it was even more freezing.

The one redeeming feature was the open fireplace still in

use, so at least we could light a fire. Or so we thought. We bought logs and laid them in the fireplace, we put a match to light them. Nothing. We tried again. We sat in our overcoats, four of us wondering why this fire would not catch. It was time to call in the churchwarden. David, a retired farmer, came and showed us how to lay a fire, first with newspaper, then kindling wood, and finally the logs; it would be even better if we could add some coal and better still if we included fire-lighters in the mix. And so, this is how we learned the noble art of lighting a fire, which can be both a deeply meditative, yet also highly frustrating experience, depending on the outcome. This was the first lesson I learned as a new vicar. It is a skill we have made good use of over the years. I was to learn later that when David returned home to his wife he said, 'Those two really are townies.' It wasn't a compliment.

Eleven years were spent in those Warwickshire villages. They formed a rich tapestry of baptisms, weddings, funerals, Remembrance Day services, Millennium celebrations and family life. The first time I was asked to baptise a baby took me by surprise. Not because I hadn't baptised babies before, the difference this time, I was the one to decide whether to do it or not. There was not higher authority to defer to, it was my decision.

One peculiarity of the church's year is the timing of Easter. I learned early on, thanks to a Catholic school education, that Easter Sunday is the first Sunday after the first full moon after the 21st March. It is a fact that has stayed with me over the years and something that is recalled whenever I'm asked why Easter Sunday seems so changeable, sometimes early, other times late in the season. When Easter is early it affects all other church planning. For instance, Mothering Sunday, which falls on the fourth Sunday of Lent is determined by the date of

Easter. Some years it can feel like you hardly catch your breath after Christmas when Easter turns up.

In 1997 Easter was early. I had been in post barely three months when Mothering Sunday came round, consequently I hadn't fully understood the regular pattern of services. It had escaped me that on the second Sunday of the month, Matins was the order of the day. This service from the book of Common Prayer, appeals to the more traditional members of a congregation. Sure enough, Mothering Sunday fell on the second Sunday of March that year. All my history of Mothering Sunday Services dictated that this should be a family service at which daffodils are handed out to all the women in the congregation. Unfortunately, as this was the Sunday for Matins, all the younger people and families stayed away. This was not good. I had prepared a lively service of guitar-led action songs and daffodils, even my 16-year-old daughter was roped into leading the classic children's song, 'The wise man built his house upon the rock'. The congregation was not amused.

After the service, two things happened. The first, a member of the choir asked me if other churches did services like this. I assured her they did. The second was more painful. Two days after the offending service I received a registered letter from a parishioner who expressed his absolute horror at such a service taking place in his church, and that he would no longer be attending, I was hurt and angry, not least for my daughter. I wanted to retaliate with, 'How many other 16 years olds would be willing to stand up in this dreary church and perform?' It would have been wise to have visited this man, listen to his complaint, and offer some calming words. I did none of this, I was too afraid of being stung again with criticism.

There were to be other similar showdowns during my time there. They were not easy years. But there was movement and growth both spiritually and in numbers.

The annual Remembrance Service attracted most of the village community and the attendance of soldiers on parade from the local army base added gravitas to the day. I never quite got used to the colonel saluting when he met me, I'm pretty sure I blushed. The same colonel invited me to join them at the Officer's Mess for a traditional Remembrance Sunday curry lunch. An afternoon of generous hospitality followed during which copious amounts of red wine were consumed. It was glorious and the first of many splendid visits to the officer's mess. There were perks to being a parish vicar.

Family life was eventful during those years. After just one year in post, Ian, who was still teaching in inner-city Birmingham, had a heart attack. Out of the blue, one February half term, he collapsed in the kitchen. Ian was rushed to hospital and in swift progression he underwent heart by-pass surgery. Fragile weeks of convalescence followed, until eventually, Ian was able to make a full recovery. But the shock of this untimely event fractured my own mental frailty, and a residual anxiety that it may happen again, stayed with me for much longer. Somehow, I had to carry on as vicar, there was no-one to take over. During the most testing time of my faith, I still had to support others with theirs.

A few weeks later, in the week before Easter, there were widespread storms and flooding which added to the stress. First there was a funeral in church, but the planned burial could not take place because the grave was full of water! We would return the next day. That same evening, at the Methodist church, I attended an ecumenical supper followed by a service for Maundy Thursday. As we were about to finish, a distraught woman arrived explaining that because most of the roads were closed due to flooding, it had taken her family hours to travel to get this far. Seeing the lights were still on in church, the woman had taken her chance and came looking for help. While we talked, she explained how frightened she had become not knowing the area or where to go. The light still on in church offered a beacon of hope and safety. This was my tipping point, the trauma of past weeks, and the trauma of that day's funeral, both took their toll. An added anxiety was the fact that my younger daughter being unable to get home from school because of flooding, thankfully she had been able to stay with a friend. I broke down, I could hold it no longer. I felt so alone.

Feeling alone is a common experience for parish clergy. In most parish churches, the vicar is the only paid member of the church. There is no team to share ideas with, no work colleague to share the load. Over the years I have had many willing volunteers, I give thanks for them often as I remember them. But unlike others who get to go home after a day's work, a vicar lives in the community where she works, even her home is the property of the church.

After nine years it was time to think about where to go next, our two daughters had flown the nest, one still at university, the other to work in the United States. The church was growing, I could have stayed and enjoyed a quieter life and it is always difficult to know when the right time to move is. But I felt I had done all I could in this parish, and a different hand was needed to steer the church into the next chapter. I was ready for a new challenge, a new adventure.

I forgot the cautionary note: 'Be careful what you wish for.'

Chapter Seven

BI-POLAR EXPRESS

It was at this point, the point at which I broke down, when life took a new turn. Mental illness struck. The stress I had been under, took its toll. So I made an appointment to see my GP to ask for a referral to a psychiatrist as a private patient. I don't know now why I didn't ask for an appointment on the NHS. I felt like one of those patients who are not quite ill enough to alert free mental health care, but I had an intuition, a gut feeling that I was not as well as I could be, so I elected to pay for a private consultation. It wasn't cheap.

I sat in the psychiatrist's office, mid-afternoon on a summer's day, listening carefully as the psychiatrist gave me her conclusion.

'Well, it's bipolar disorder, type II,' she stated.

'Are you sure?' I asked.

'Almost certainly,' came the reply.

I remember there being a stillness in the air, and I felt a sense of relief. Perhaps that's a strange thing to say; why would

I have felt relief when receiving this verdict about the state of my mental health? I was no stranger to matters of mental ill-health, for years I had been prone to anxiety and depression. Medication had helped, but I had never felt fully recovered. Depression hadn't caused me to have much time off work, most of the time I had managed, sometimes struggling in despair as the weight of suppressed emotions lay heavy on my soul. This new diagnosis gave a language to a mental image that I carried in my psyche. I somehow knew that my depression was not typical, I didn't slide into a deep slump and stay there, though there were occasional episodes like that. No, my experience was more of a yo-yo effect. I felt like I was a ball bouncing between the polarities which would usually end with the highs eventually losing their bounce, giving way to the gravity of the lows. For years I had tried to describe this mental image to a variety of GPs, and though I received kindness and anti-depressants I was never sure they knew what I was talking about. I didn't know what I was talking about. So, a diagnosis of bi-polar disorder, albeit the lesser type II, made perfect sense to me.

This psychiatrist, a woman, younger than me, was polished, professional, and not without empathy; she listened with care as I described my symptoms. Her office was furnished with an uncluttered simplicity, it was unlike any other clinical situation I had been in. Though I felt calm, I also felt inferior, and I was desperate to be a good, compliant patient.

I had started to experience clinical depression during the early years of life as an ordained minister in the Church of England. My GP at the time spoke of depression as an imbalance of chemicals in the brain that needed to be remedied with medication. It sounded plausible, who was I to know differently? My doctor was keen to assure me that there was nothing to be ashamed of when suffering with depression. He also set up some counselling sessions and I was fortunate to receive more than one referral to a counsellor courtesy of the NHS. This was the mid-1990s, I doubt that would be so available today.

The wide variety of counsellors I have met with over the years certainly fulfilled the brief to do no harm. Some were helpful and insightful, but in all cases, the positive outcome was short lived. I would feel supported during a period of struggle or crisis but somewhere deep inside of me I sensed there was something missing. I felt as though I was being propped up like a building whose foundations were crumbling when what I really needed was someone to take a more forensic intervention into what lay beneath.

For years I had explored many avenues trying to find something or someone that would make me feel better. The Church of England has some resources available to its clergy, medical personnel who will offer a consultancy, free of charge, thus short circuiting longer waiting lists. I had met one such consultant psychiatrist some years earlier. He was an interesting character who took pinches of snuff during our sessions! The diagnosis was the same, depression, with yet another new drug to try, though he did say something that helped. With a broad Scottish brogue, he proclaimed: 'Depression is not a moral issue, my dear.'

It wasn't my fault.

In time, I would learn that what lay beneath these episodes of depression, were corrosive beliefs about not being good enough and fears of abandonment and rejection. No wonder I felt the emptiness of depression. But for now, I welcomed this new diagnosis of type II bi-polar disorder. Now, finally, there was a new name to put to my feelings and with it a new remedy. This new diagnosis made sense to me because another mental image I carried in my head was of being on a seesaw, going up and down, constantly trying to arrive at an equilibrium. Up to that point, I had functioned well enough on a daily anti-depressant. But even in my best moments, the feeling that unhappiness lay lurking just beneath the surface was never far away.

One time when sitting alone in my parish office, with feelings of despair and hopelessness at a peak, I cried out to God: 'Please send someone to help me.' That prayer would be answered one day. But at that point of desperation, I found care and compassion in the company of my local GP who listened carefully and renewed my prescription for anti-depressants. He was doing all he could to help me.

Apart from my own personal struggles I didn't mind admitting to depression and a diagnosis of bi-polar disorder when I needed to, because I was in secure employment. I held the living as vicar of two parishes which meant I pretty much had a job for life if I wanted it. Without some act of gross misbehaviour, my job was secure, and being part of an institution where pastoral care was a core condition, there shouldn't have been a problem. There wasn't then, but I found out to my cost that once I left the safe harbour of my secure parish position, things would become very different.

But let's not get ahead of the story, let's stay with the diagnosis: bipolar disorder type II. As I said, initially I was relieved, I reasoned that maybe now there would be a way out of this prison. Perhaps there would be some remedy, a magic bullet that would rescue me from feeling like I was being haunted. So, my new psychiatrist prescribed another drug to accompany the anti-depressant I was already taking, this time a mood stabiliser. She presented me with an invoice for the consultation, pausing momentarily to check if I was covered by private insurance and mildly surprised to see that I was not. In response I wrote a cheque for a significant sum of money and arranged to see her one month later.

When I left her office, I returned to the everyday of finding my parked car to make my way home. It hadn't occurred to me for a moment to question the diagnosis, even less to consider why I might have this ongoing lingering depression and whether there might be causes other than genetics. With a new medication written on the familiar green prescription paper, I made my way to the pharmacy. I thought to myself: 'This time, this time, things will start to get better.'

It was expensive seeing a psychiatrist in private practice, but I was willing to pay if it meant there would be a way to get off this bi-polar express train.

Much later I had a dream about polar bears. In the dream they were getting in the way of me trying to exit a holiday camp. I knew they were dangerous and so I was afraid to move, I was trapped. It was as though whatever was happening to me psychologically, I was being held back.

Chapter Eight

PARIS

I settled down to parish life again with the new regime of medication that helped bring a measure of calm to me. But the urge to move on to somewhere new, returned. In the autumn of 2008, I applied for a job in Paris, and was appointed as an associate chaplain at an Anglican church there. I had wanted to work in France for a long time. Having lived in Switzerland, all those years ago, I had been looking-for a chance to live and work in a French speaking country.

I was a Francophile, and over the years, I visited France many times for holidays. Ian and I also got to spend three months in France enjoying a sabbatical from parish ministry. Thanks to a working agreement between the Church of England and the French Reformed Church, I was able to visit colleagues who ministered in Compiegne, Nice, Bergerac and Alsace. For one month we luxuriated in the Dordogne, which must be the gourmet food capital of France. The whole trip took place during the glorious summer months and long days of May, June and July. This was a much-needed chance to really unwind.

One evening during this trip, we were dining out at a typically rustic local restaurant, whose strap line should be, 'Never knowingly underfeeds his customers'. We arrived back to where we were staying at 10pm, to a still sunlit sky, and decided that as we were far too full to contemplate sleep, we would do the laundry. The washing machine was located across the courtyard. Two hours later, when it was pitch black, as it was now midnight, we stumbled giggling and inebriated, retrieving the clothes, and hanging them on the clothesline.

During this time, I was able to brush up on my French courtesy of attendance at Mass at the local Roman Catholic church. I made two discoveries there. First, the liturgy was familiar, almost identical, which made the language easy to understand; this also made me question why our two churches, Anglican and Roman Catholic are divided. The second was a delight, I realised that I would still be a Christian even if I wasn't paid to be! That was quite a moment. It was good to take part in prayer and worship without any responsibility for anyone else's spiritual life.

From the sublime to the ridiculous, the house where we stayed had a private swimming pool, so here I swam naked for the first and only time in my life. This memory of a hot July day, lingers, not least because moments after I left the pool, the gardener appeared.

There was one more French experience that fanned the flame of my desire to live and work in France. My father had been a Normandy Veteran, and my mother had continued an association with the local branch after my father's death. Every year, around D-Day, she would make a pilgrimage to Normandy and on the 69th anniversary, and I was invited to accompany the branch as Chaplain.

So, when the chance came to live and work in France as associate chaplain at a large Anglican Chaplaincy, it felt like a divine plan. When I think about it now, I see that the signs of disaster were present before I even started. But when it seems that the dream job has come along, you don't see beyond that hope.

After eleven secure years in my post as vicar, I was ready for a change. I wasn't getting any younger so if I was going to make this bold move into a new life it seemed the time to do it. I brushed off the problem that there was no offer of accommodation. I ignored the feeling that things couldn't be quite right if I was expected to find somewhere to live ready for a September start. It felt as though no-one on the staff really understood the challenges I faced. But I was undaunted, so eager to start this new adventure.

In the winter of 2008, we moved into the garage of a parishioner, which was to be our home until we found an apartment. Yes, that's right, we lived in the converted garage of a church member who lived at least one hour's commute out of Paris. How lucky was I?

Eventually we found an apartment we could just about afford with the meagre housing allowance that came with the job, and we were able to move our belongings out of our roomy south Warwickshire vicarage into a two-bedroomed apartment in the 16th district of Paris. This is the enviable district of Paris; we were in the down-at-heel end.

After some serious downsizing to fit into our new residence, our remaining worldly good arrived. The narrow streets of Paris aren't built for ease of passage of a huge removal van. On the day we moved into our apartment, two plucky removal men rode up and down in a Parisian two-person lift, carrying our furniture. Now we were all set.

The pace of my new life began straight away. With no time to settle in and adjust, the chaplain told us to make our way to central Paris to help transport people to a rural location for our chaplaincy weekend away. None of us knew exactly how to get there but we did our best to negotiate Paris in the Friday rush hour traffic and make our way to Nevers, in central France.

It turned out to be a great weekend; we had finally arrived and were at the heart of chaplaincy life. I learned the etiquette of Parisian life, courtesy of a talk on the subject. We were getting to know people who went to the church, and we, too, were becoming known and accepted. On the Saturday night, there was karaoke. I love karaoke, I come into my own at Karaoke! I jumped at the chance to sing 'Don't go breaking my heart', the classic Kiki Dee and Elton John number. If only I had known how prophetic that song would be.

Life as an associate chaplain began. The Paris Metro in the rush hour, became my daily commute, a crushing experience of too many bodies in a confined space. Our local stations were Exelmans and Port St. Cloud, and even the short walk to and from these stations involved a careful negotiation around dog poo and beggars. The long days were filled with meetings, planning and navigating the politics of the chaplaincy team, which comprised an administrator, an assistant minister, two interns with responsibility for youth ministry and me, I was the newbie.

Life was difficult. When a newcomer joins a group that has been together for a while, as this staff team had, it is good practice to re-form. My expectation was that introductions would be made with roles and expectations clarified. That didn't happen. Still, I contributed my thoughts and opinions in the way I saw others doing. I see now, in hindsight, that I should have kept quiet and observed the dynamics in play, while working out who really had the power. Before long, I sensed a growing resentment towards me among some of the staff, which I ignored to my cost. My occasional returns to the UK for my counselling training courses were barely tolerated, even though they had been agreed at my interview. My presence seemed to unsettle staff meetings, not least when I was asked to speak about a project, I felt no one was listening.

One time I was despatched to console Jill a member of the congregation who had been upset by one of the young interns. The intern, Sophia, had arrived at the staff meeting in tears because she reported that Jill had been unkind to her. I met with Jill and reported back to the team as requested, and I was not prepared to stay silent as Sophia continued to blame Jill for the conflict. Sophia became tearful again, and the chaplain turned on me with these words, 'Stop being horrible to Sophia!' I had become piggy in the middle, or more accurately, the scape goat. I was to learn that blaming a third party rather than dealing with the issue at hand was the toxic pattern. I realised, too late, that no-one had my back. The experience triggered a deep sense of abandonment in me, and had it been an isolated incident I might have survived. But it wasn't and I didn't.

The dynamics at work were hurtful and I was finding life increasingly more difficult and unpredictable; it was stressful, but I was not aware of how it was affecting me, I was so keen to make this new role work. I had given up so much for this, as had my long-suffering husband. Living and working in France was a long-time dream but it was becoming a nightmare. My emotions were becoming unstable. Things came to a head one fateful day. In the hope of improving the deteriorating relationship between myself and my supervisor, I disclosed that I was living with a diagnosis of bi-polar disorder, though I stressed it was being well managed. I said I was sorry if my reactions to some events seemed out of proportion. I thought if I owned my part in the discomfort it would help, but I discovered later, to my cost, that it would be held against me.

I wonder now if that is a female response. It certainly was my tendency, to internalise the blame in the hope that everything would be alright. I didn't realise that I was the only one doing this. No-one stepped forward to offer me support or guidance, not even a cautionary word about how I might handle things differently. I think the die had already been cast.

Paris was not a total disaster; I met some very interesting people and enjoyed some success as a minister. I had only been there three weeks when it occurred to me that pastoral ministry is very similar wherever it takes place, in the end it's about the one-to-one encounters with individuals who come seeking a listening ear and a heart that cares. The difference in an overseas chaplaincy is that people may be around for only a very short while, even just a weekend. One such weekend visitor was a young man who approached me at the end of the service I had just led. He asked me to bless the wedding ring, bought for his intended wife. I felt honoured. I shared this with the chaplain, he smiled. I wonder now if he was jealous that I had been approached rather than him. It was this smile that I came to recognise as a cover for deeper feelings of resentment, even jealousy. Another time, I found myself conducting a service of Holy Communion for a Sinhalese community. These gracious people were so welcoming and delighted to meet this new minister, assuring me that they would carry out a line-by-line translation of the liturgy. It was a relief; my Sinhalese is non-existent.

Members of the congregation ranged in social status from the extremely well-off banking executive, used to spending hundreds of pounds on wine collecting, to the down-at-heel almost homeless person. It was from the former that I learned that wine originating from the Languedoc region in France was a good buy, because it had quality but was lesser known, so it could be bought at a reasonable price. Equally, spending time with expatriate Americans in the season of Thanksgiving produced an invitation to a wonderful Thanksgiving dinner, two days after the official date. In the United States, Thanksgiving Day is a public holiday and falls on the last Thursday in November. This means that expat Americans around the world usually celebrate their national feast two days later at the weekend.

In the main, I found myself involved with people at the poorer end of the spectrum; people like the lonely widow who had married a French man but was now quite alone in a foreign country. Also, there were the students or au pairs still finding their feet far from home. Perhaps that, too, was a problem, I was being well received and liked by the ones who had little power or status and increasingly looked down on by long-standing members of wealth and influence.

Ian had already retired by the time we moved to Paris, which made the move possible, and whilst not a French speaker, he threw himself into church life in Paris with enthusiasm. Ian is a good cook so when a chef was needed to provide dinner for the weekly bible study, he stepped up to the task. One shopping trip, to buy twenty chicken legs, exposed his lack of French, as he had completely forgotten the French for chicken. He had to resort to mime. A career as a teacher had given him a resourceful edge, so he pointed to his thighs and began impersonating a chicken! I wish I had been there. Ian's warmth of personality and willing spirit won him many friends.

Our time in Paris didn't end well for me. One evening I was summoned to a meeting of the chaplain, two wardens and the treasurer, to learn I was being summarily dismissed. I received no notice and already the Sunday duties I had been preparing had been handed over to someone else. And though it wasn't cited as the reason, my disclosure of a diagnosis of bi-polar disorder some weeks earlier, had been shared with others. I felt a huge sense of betrayal at the time, but nothing prepared me for the shock of this meeting.

With the words, 'we have made a mistake', I was told I would receive three months' salary but was expected to leave immediately and cautioned not to speak to anyone at church. It dawned on me very slowly that though the job had been offered to me by the most senior person present at the meeting with the words, 'I look forward to having an experienced colleague working alongside me', the last thing that had been wanted was an experienced, opinionated woman colleague. That same senior person, my colleague, did not speak, nor has he spoken to me since. This experience has not hindered his progress.

I had no right of redress. I was completely shattered, stunned, speechless.

When Ian came to meet me from work, having just carried out another errand on behalf of the chaplaincy, he found me unable to speak, I couldn't find the words to explain to him what had happened, simply that we had to leave quickly because I didn't want to break down in tears while I was still on the premises.

The next day, we left for the UK for our post-Christmas break; fortunately for the chaplain, he had already had his, which made sure that I was still in post so that his holiday plans were not disrupted.

Chapter Nine

AFTERMATH

What are we going to do? We are about to become homeless? What did I do wrong? These were the questions that ran through my mind as we left Paris. I had to find another job. As a priest in the Church of England our home was dependent on my position as vicar. For many years, we had lived in 'tied accommodation', like all clergy, since ordination I had lived in the house that went with the job. But now, I would be unemployed so where would we live and how was I to get a job and a home having just been sacked? Would I now be seen as a problem and would my eleven years as a vicar count for nothing?

We drove back to England from Paris for my post-Christmas break and the shock and suddenness of what had just happened stunned me into silence. Ian drove to Calais for the ferry, and I sat in the passenger seat pale and uncommunicative. My whole life had been turned upside down, our whole life had been disrupted and it felt like it was all my fault.

Thankfully, Ian didn't blame me, and he could only look on helplessly as I endured the sense of shame and failure that washed over me.

I can't remember now what prompted me to return to my former Bishop, though I knew I had to go somewhere to begin to pick up the pieces. This Bishop had been supportive of me and my ministry; he was always someone I could sit with and speak to honestly. Perhaps as he knew enough about my former ministry, he would give me the benefit of the doubt regarding Paris. I phoned his secretary to make an appointment to see him.

I was nervous as I approached his familiar home, but my fears were allayed when I heard the words, 'welcome home' and felt a warm embrace before he ushered me into his office. The Bishop and his Archdeacon had heard what had happened to me. Thank God both clergymen had a good opinion of me, and both assured me that what had happened to me in Paris was not my fault; I began to gather the fragments of my life and ministry and rebuild some semblance of self-respect. The Bishop asked if I wanted my old job back as they hadn't yet filled the vacancy. I didn't think this was a serious offer, so I declined. The reasons for not entertaining the idea of returning to my former parish were complex; in the first place I felt a sense of shame, having left one ministry in joyful anticipation of a life and ministry in France. I didn't know how I would face my former parishioners. I also had a deeper gut feeling that if it felt right to leave those parishes, because I genuinely believed I had done all I could do for them, then it was right that someone new take over, nothing had changed, that was still true.

I've thought about this in the years that have passed since making that decision. Was it pride or a misplaced sense of vocation that stopped me considering a return to my former parishes? There was still the drive to move forwards to something new, I didn't consider for a moment that a return to my old job could have been just a temporary measure, which would have given me security for a while and time to consider more carefully the way ahead.

The meeting with the Bishop concluded with a measure of confidence restored and at least the security of knowing that, when I applied for other posts, there would be someone who would validate my ministerial record and give me a reference. The job hunting began in earnest. Applications were made from our apartment in Paris, after all we had nowhere else to live, and the severance package I received covered the rent on our apartment for a few more months. It wasn't very long before I was offered another position as vicar of two parishes in the Midlands.

However, the long arm of the Church of England reaches far and the sense of relief at securing future employment and somewhere to live was soon overshadowed by another Bishop.

An unexpected phone call from his secretary invited me with Ian to meet my new Diocesan Bishop. I went along, I assumed that it would be a courtesy meeting as we had not met previously. The last thing I expected was to be ambushed, again. As we entered the Bishop's office, I was surprised to see that there was someone else present to take notes. Introductions had hardly begun when I was confronted with a question about my diagnosis of bi-polar disorder. The Bishop demanded to know why I hadn't declared it at my interview. My inner world began to collapse, but an early survival technique kicked in, the ability to think on my feet. I replied, 'Because I know the discrimination there is about mental illness.'

As the questioning continued, it became clear that all the ethical and transparent routes around employment law had been bypassed, enquiries had been made about me without my knowledge or consent. Not only that, other issues from my past ministerial record were laid out before me, such as a difficult relationship with a former curate. I was quick to point out that all those involved at a senior level had recognised it was not my fault. Fear began to rise, was I going to lose this job before I had even begun? Where would we live? Was this more abandonment, more rejection?

I was angry, but I dared not show it otherwise it might confirm the suspicions he already had about me. At a gut level I knew this was unethical and unfair, I had been found guilty before I even had the chance to put my case forward. It was clear he had spoken to people in Paris, but I didn't know to who or what had been asked.

'But these are good people Charmaine,' the Bishop said of the people he had spoken to. Who were these people? Sadly, the 'good people' belief has been used many times to hide or defend the abuse of power. Later, I would reflect on the nature of the church and wonder how it behaved as an institution. And I wish I had answered the Bishop with this, 'And your point, Bishop?' But for now, all my survival instincts came to the fore, and I complied with all that was being asked of me.

My disillusion with the Church's hierarchy began that day.

The result was that I didn't lose the job, but the terms of my employment were drastically changed in such a way that my start in the new parishes would be skewed from the beginning. The churchwardens would be informed that I was being put in post for a year with the licence 'priest-in-charge' rather than vicar and after this my role as vicar would be confirmed.

The role of vicar in any church is dependent on trust, the

trust of the people in their new minister and the trust of the minister in their congregation and their senior diocesan clergy. In one fell swoop trust was shattered. Churchwardens were asking themselves, 'What's wrong with our new vicar that her terms of engagement have been changed?' And how could I answer this in any way that would not show me in a bad light? What made matters worse, the parishes I was going to, had a reputation of being difficult. A small number of people had regularly written to the Bishop complaining about the vicar before me, whoever he had been. Not to mention that some were adamantly opposed to the ordination of women so would vehemently object to any woman priest being put in post.

Perhaps it was this that caused my new Bishop to be anxious. It is possible that he was concerned for my welfare when he discovered that I had received a diagnosis of bi-polar disorder. But it didn't feel like that when he sent me to see a consultant psychiatrist, it felt like I was being checked out rather than supported.

The night the Bishop came to install me as priest in charge, of my new parishes, he gave me a bottle of fine red wine and said, 'I think we got off on the wrong foot.' I wanted to reply, 'Yes, we did, but it is going to affect me and my life here much more than yours'. But I didn't say those things, instead I just smiled to make it easier for all of us and I tried to put it all out of my mind, as I was keen to make a fresh start. The familiar habit of internalising the awkwardness, kicked in. The licencing went as well as these things do with a church full of people keen to see who the new vicar is, most of whom would rarely return to church again. A few days later, the Bishop phoned me. He had clearly reflected on my situation and maybe realised he had been less than helpful, because he went on to tell me about the Diocesan Counselling Scheme for clergy. He told me that a certain number of sessions would be available to me free of charge. He assured me that this was a confidential service and would provide an opportunity to process all that had happened in Paris. I was grateful for this prompt because if I was to resume my own counselling training, I would have to find someone to continue my own therapeutic process.

It is never easy to find a therapist. And now I was in a new situation not knowing anyone, it was good to have the field narrowed down by accessing this diocesan network of counsellors. I leafed through the diocesan booklet, all the names were unknown to me, except one. One name stood out; he had been recommended by a friend. So, when I met John and he asked me, 'Why therapy, why now?' I answered, 'The Bishop sent me.'

Part Two

Chapter Ten

INTRODUCTION TO THERAPY

If you hadn't found me, Charmaine, you would have
been very ill by now.

These words shocked me. They were a reality check; I was in
therapy, not because of some self-indulgent whim, nor because
I was fascinated by my weekly encounter with this separate
other, but because I needed to be.

I found my way to the therapist who spoke those words
through a recommendation from a friend. She knew how
bruised I had felt after my experience in Paris. She sensed I
would benefit from therapy with this psychotherapist, and I
would learn in time that this one would be different from
others I had known.

Along with the encouragement from the Bishop, I was

required to go into therapy because I had resumed training as a counsellor. The hidden gift of training to be a counsellor is the requirement to have your own therapy, so that you become aware of your own psychological makeup before trying to help a client with theirs. I didn't welcome this requirement; it would be costly. But in the end, it was the most helpful thing I did as a trainee counsellor. As it turned out, it was one of the most valuable things I have ever done in life.

My motivation towards training to be a counsellor was twofold. After many years of parish ministry, I knew I needed to find a way to grow as a person. I had become weary with all my conversations centring on matters to do with the church. If I met someone for the first time and they discovered I was a priest, they would often begin with the reasons they didn't go to church. Alternatively, they might start to ask me wider questions about the institution. A local favourite was to ask why the church was selling off the neighbourhood allotments.

With my own parishioners there might be complaints about what I was failing to do as a vicar, but there were also times when I was told how well I was doing, and how much I was appreciated. When the BBC series 'The Vicar of Dibley' was first broadcast, an enthusiastic neighbour stopped me in the street to tell me how much she enjoyed the programme, and how like me the character was! I was flattered, but also a little alarmed. Years later, when on a routine visit, my GP asked what my profession was. I said, 'I'm a vicar.' There was a moment's pause. 'Oh,' he said. 'I was only talking to my housemate last night who told me he had never seen "The Vicar of Dibley". We're going to watch it tonight.' Another pause before I responded, 'You do know she is not a real vicar, don't you? I on the other hand am a real vicar.'

So, training to be a counsellor was my attempt at finding a

place where I could learn about myself as a person when I was not 'the woman vicar'.

The second reason I began serious training to be a counsellor was because of a family member's illness. I had seen at close quarters how mental ill-health can strike out of the blue and how we could do better both as a society and as a church to promote good mental health. My first-hand experience of mental ill-health spurred me on to train so that I could offer one small drop of healing into an ocean of brokenness.

By the time I met John, I was no stranger to therapy. Over the years I had seen a variety of counsellors who had helped me at different stages of my life, some of whom had been better than others. Most had offered a degree of help or comfort during periods of depression and self-doubt. I had received predominantly person-centred counselling; a modality which puts the emphasis on the client leading the work. A person-centred counsellor will have as their core values: empathy, unconditional positive regard and congruence.

I also had received a short period of Cognitive Behavioural Therapy (CBT), courtesy of my local GP. This was fine at first. However, after the initial session, the approach did not work for me, and over the years, I've wondered about this. Was the modality the problem for me, or was it seeing a counsellor at the GP surgery that was the issue? I think it was both. The power dynamic at the GP surgery works in favour of the professional, this is understandable when seeing a doctor. It works less well when it comes to seeing a counsellor. CBT, as I understand it, invites the patient to examine their thought processes and then consider why they may think the way they do. I think this approach already requires a certain amount of self-awareness or mental wellness, and for me it hooked into a habitual pattern of feeling that I had to 'please the expert' or comply with a parent figure.

Despite my experience with counselling, I still had no real idea about the fragility of my mental health. The therapist I met was John, a clergyman.

I have known many clergy, mostly men, long enough to also know that they come in many shapes and sizes. Nevertheless, when I first met John, he took me completely by surprise. I had expected an elderly man, white haired, black shirted, wearing a clerical collar. I didn't expect to meet someone wearing jeans and a fleece, someone close to my age.

This first visit became the first of countless visits to see this therapist.

We had already spoken before this first meeting. When I had phoned him for an appointment, I had been greeted by his answerphone. He had returned my call and had been greeted by mine. Eventually we had been able to talk to each other and had made our first arrangement to meet. These were the days before Google Maps, and I have never been very good at following directions, even with an AA Route Finder. So, on the way for our first meeting, I took a wrong turn on the way, got lost, and had to phone John for directions. After two more phone calls, I arrived at his house, fifteen minutes late and there he was standing in the drive to greet me with the words, 'Tea? Coffee? The loo is in there.'

I was in a bad way when I met him. Of course, I didn't know it then, but he did. And I would learn that had I not found my way to this person, my story would have taken a different turn. Or perhaps, more accurately, I would have continued along the path that was breaking me.

For years I had struggled with mental health issues, but I didn't recognise it. Sure, I'd had bouts of depression which I put down to strange brain chemistry, but I hadn't seen that my continuing battle with anxiety was not normal. I was used to a roller-coaster of emotions; I thought it was just the quirkiness of being me.

Years earlier, when I shared my feelings of emptiness with a close friend, he replied, 'You're fine Charmaine.' I believed him, but deep down I knew I was not.

By the time I met John I had come to terms with a daily routine of taking anti-depressants, to which my psychiatrist had added a mood-stabiliser along with the diagnosis of bi-polar disorder. I had been on a twenty-year journey of battling feelings of despair and dread. I could overcome these ghosts when I was highly stimulated and energised, but I knew at my core there was a vulnerability to a seeping sadness and weariness that was often overwhelming.

I would be reminded of this from time to time, especially when I questioned whether it was still ok to be seeing a thera-pist. This reality check reminded me that I was here for heal-ing. Psychotherapy literally means 'therapy of the soul'.

But John's style of therapy was not textbook therapy. You're not really supposed to say to your client: 'If you hadn't found me, you would be very ill by now.' It would almost certainly be frowned upon in client-led person-centred circles. This therapist was different. I observed many times over, that of his many gifts, the most profound was the freedom he felt to depart from the textbooks for the sake of what he discerned his client needed.

Our meetings were weekly, in his office, which was a protected space where a therapeutic relationship could grow. Here, I was not someone's wife, mother, daughter, sister, friend or vicar; I was learning who it was, to be Charmaine. This learning would happen in the context of relating to another human being, who had the skill to listen to me with compassion and hear the pain that had never fully been expressed.

There are many stereotypes about therapists and therapeutic spaces. Neutrality is encouraged, with little evidence of the counsellor's real life. I have sat with different counsellors in rooms that are decorated in muted colours, simply furnished with one or two tasteful pictures on the wall. Occasionally, I have been alarmed to be in a therapy room that had a couch, though was never invited to use it! This time I was sat in a working study surrounded by bookshelves laden with books on theology and psychotherapy; many of which I recognised. On the desk sat a computer where sermons were written, and emails dealt with. It was a familiar setting. The walls were decorated with pictures, some John had painted, some were photographs. Once in a while we discussed the latest photographs one of us had taken, as I, too, am a keen photographer. It was a protected space, and I felt secure.

That first session, so many years ago now, is etched on my mind, imprinted in my psyche. As I began to tell my story I noticed that John was turning to the side with his eyes closed. That's strange, I thought, isn't a good counsellor supposed to look at you while they are listening? I asked John about this many years later, and his reply didn't surprise me. He told me that he could hear the screaming, he could hear the cry of the inner child who had waited so long for someone to listen to her.

Chapter Eleven

A BUCKET OF COLD WATER

The first meeting with a counsellor is an important one, it is where client and therapist are weighing each other up, finding out whether they can work together. For most people, going to see a therapist is a huge step which requires a great act of courage. Because I had seen a counsellor before, and as a trainee myself, this part didn't worry me. I knew that both of us would be taking a risk. Though I wasn't quite ready when, during our first session John said, 'I wish I had a bucket of cold water in the corner, I'd throw it over you to wake you up.' My first thoughts were: Is he supposed to say that? What does he mean? Where is the warm empathic response? Nevertheless, I was curious about how I was presenting. Did I seem switched off? Was my inner life so closed that I looked like I was falling asleep? I told my tutor about this the next time I saw her as I wasn't quite sure if it was an acceptable therapeutic intervention. She looked at me wryly and said, 'Oh I think you're going to have a lot of fun with this one.'

Neither was I quite prepared the time he said, 'Be careful who you bring in here, this is between you and me.' What did he mean by that? I wondered.

Over time we would get to know each other, and in this relationship of trust, my way of being in the world would begin to show. The cautionary note about not bringing other people into the space was to guard against any tendency I might have of talking about other people when things became challenging or uncomfortable. Sometimes it's much easier to talk about someone else's problems rather than face our own. 'This is between you and me,' he said, and it was.

In the therapy world there are, quite rightly, many and frequent conversations about ethics and appropriate behaviour between counsellor and client. Questions are asked about touch. For instance, should the therapist shake hands with the client? What about contact between sessions? Can the client email or phone the therapist? Can a counsellor and client care for each other? I have heard counsellor colleagues say that you can be an adequate counsellor without caring for the client, but I wonder how effective therapy is without a degree of caring for the wounded person who comes hoping to find help with her or his distress.

Much is written about dependency. Therapists can become anxious about the client becoming too dependent on them, but isn't the historic lack of a dependable care giver the reason a person finds themselves in therapy?

I went through phases of great dependency in my therapy, which John tolerated. This sometimes-meant frequent phone calls and email exchanges. Somehow, he managed to hold the boundaries of our relationship that enabled my growth towards healing. The sense I had was that I was cared for, and this was the key to unlocking the prison vaults of my being.

Put simply, my therapeutic journey was only made possible because I believed that I mattered to this person, even though I questioned it many times.

So here I was, the first session with a psychotherapist. He asked me why I had come, why now. I began the story of Paris.

As I recounted my experience of Paris, I felt defensive, afraid that my new therapist would think it was really all my fault and that somehow, I was defective and deserved to be fired. It would take some time before I really believed that there was no judgement in the therapist's office. I didn't use the chaplain's name, I still felt a kind of misplaced loyalty towards him, as though I should protect his reputation. I felt the same about other senior ecclesiastical personnel, until the moment John asked why I should pay such attention to authority figures when they hadn't done me any favours. Already there were the seeds of what would be major issues to explore: how I felt about authority and paternal figures.

By the end of our first session, which passed by in a flash, we agreed that, yes, we could get along together. We agreed to meet every week on Thursdays at 3pm. This would be my time, my protected hour. When I returned home, I started to tell Ian, about the session. As I did so, I began to weep. Deep sobbing continued, and Ian could only sit and listen. I couldn't explain why I was weeping; I didn't know myself. To his credit he didn't try to soothe or resolve my distress, he simply maintained his presence with me. To this day I am grateful for this. There would be many more occasions when this quality of presence was called upon. The following Thursday I told John what had happened, and his response was simply, 'The healing work has begun.'

There was sometimes a certain arrogance about John which amused me and had the effect of working his way into my affections. After the first session, he told me that this was the first vacancy he had had for two years so God must already be on the case. He also told me that he would 'get my power back' and that he had had a lot of success. I loved this. It is quite outrageous to present yourself so confidently as a therapist, there are many discussions that we could have about the ethics of this approach. To me, it was reassuring. Here was someone who inspired enough confidence that he would be able to handle whatever emerged.

During the first six sessions, I began to tell my life story, so that together, John and I could look at the core beliefs I carried about myself. What lay at the root of some of the life decisions I had made? Why, for instance, did I return home from Switzerland rather than continue to push the boundaries and explore what life had in store for me? Why had I decided to pursue the route to ordination?

I was born the third of six children, the first daughter, in a working-class family whose parents worked hard in a variety of jobs that included nursing, manufacturing, postal delivery and bar work. I was brought up as a Roman Catholic attending a Catholic school, and every Sunday, I would take myself to church, a bus ride away.

The earliest image I shared with the therapist was not a memory, but something I had learned from family story telling. Shortly after my birth, my father was off work with a back injury which resulted in him being in a plaster cast and confined to bed. At the same time, my mother returned to work as an industrial nurse, and I have never known whether it was because we needed the income or because she wanted to resume her profession; I suspect it was both. She worked nights. This meant that I spent long hours as a young baby in the care of a disabled man, lying next to him in bed. My father would reminisce about those times; his memory was that I was no trouble, I lay content. My mother was absent, either because she was working nights or, of necessity, sleeping during the day.

John reacted to this by saying, 'Oh that sounds like quite a cute picture.' I was surprised because I had always suspected this was not quite how it should be for a newborn baby. Intuitively I knew there was something wrong with this. Later in our time together I asked John about his reaction, and he answered me seriously, 'That image will stay with me until my dying day, but I knew it was too soon in our work to begin to look at it.' He knew the level of abandonment I had experienced could only be explored when we had formed a secure and solid therapeutic relationship. My experience was not being diminished, rather it was held until the time was right. John had heard the screaming.

The fear of abandonment had become a powerful driver in my life. Why would I place so much trust and power in the hands of authority figures? Because I feared abandonment. Written into my core, from the earliest time, was the experience of abandonment, of having to hold onto life in the absence of active care givers.

How did I know the truth of this? Was this just a theory I was placing on family history? I knew the truth of it because in the here and now of a therapeutic relationship it became very easy to trigger feelings of abandonment. As the bond grew between us, I became more aware when feelings of abandonment emerged.

Often during our sessions, I would start to feel an ache on the left side of my body. In the early days of my therapy, these gripping pains would run all through the left side of my chest; they were a mixture of heartache and longing. Towards the end of my therapy, they had diminished to almost nothing, just an occasional twinge in my heart, a tangible sign of the progress that had been made. Though the feelings have never quite gone away completely, these days they serve as a helpful guide. I know when I begin to have those uncomfortable feelings, I need to pay attention to what is happening to me.

My expectation of therapy was that it would soothe, relieve and bring some solution to the struggles of life. I hadn't anticipated that the journey towards healing would involve its own challenge as I confronted and walked through the historic pain, accompanied by John. He went on to explain that the aim of therapy was to create a safe space where painful memories could emerge and be held between us, so together we could look at them. We would do more than just look at them. We would listen for emotions that had never been expressed, feelings that had never been validated or given permission to exist. The months and years of therapy with John would unearth anger, jealousy, grief, lament, lost hope and much more. Love would also emerge. Nevertheless, it always felt counter intuitive to attend my weekly therapy sessions to experience and confront psychological pain, a legacy of childhood trauma.

The twin sister of abandonment is rejection, or to change the metaphor, they are like two sides of the same coin. When someone has had an early and formative experience of abandonment, they are always on the lookout for any sign of being rejected, there is a heightened alertness to anything in the present that may indicate rejection. This in turn lends itself to a fertile and febrile imagination. During the many years that I made the weekly pilgrimage to see John, the anxiety never entirely left that each time I saw him, maybe this would be the time when I was no longer welcome. At the start of the session, I would need to ground myself in the present. There were a few rituals that refreshed my memory. Holding a mug of tea in my hand, tasting the hot unsweetened liquid I would feel its warmth. Then I would focus on the pictures on the wall and feel the carpet beneath my feet. The familiar sights and sounds calmed me. One time I arrived to find that the pictures had been changed and this threw me into panic, followed by anger. How dare the familiarity of my therapeutic space be changed? It felt like something of mine had been taken away and I was not slow in expressing my anger. Times like these tested the relationship. Was it sufficiently robust to withstand the rage that would often appear with barely a moment's notice? At such times, I was aware how carefully John had worked, especially during the first two years, to establish our therapeutic alliance.

Chapter Twelve

TRANSFERENCE

While travelling home after one Thursday session, a poem came to me. I lived about an hour and a half away from John, which is quite a distance to travel on a weekly basis for a one-hour session, but I didn't mind it. Driving the familiar route towards John's office, I had time to consider what I wanted to bring to the session. The journey home gave me time to reflect and process the work we had done before I arrived home.

The poem 'Brain Freeze' came to me on one such journey home. It followed a powerful experience in therapy of emotional shut-down. I had become very still not moving for some while. I don't know for how long, but it was sufficiently long for John to bring it into awareness. He asked me to move, and I replied with a simple 'no'. We didn't unpack what had just happened, but I guess he knew, and realisation dawned for me on the way home. Words tumbled out into the poem I wrote as soon as I arrived home. I sent it to John, I wanted him to know that I understood. It was important to me that I explained what had happened. Even this action was a bid to prevent abandonment. As I reflect on this now, it occurs to me how powerfully the fear of abandonment ran within my psyche. I wanted John, as my therapist, to know I was trying my best, I wasn't being awkward, I didn't want to disappoint him.

I was experiencing a powerful transference. Something in the encounter between us had triggered an earlier experience and to this day I cannot recall what the trigger was or what was said or done, but I vividly remember the experience of sitting in a frozen state.

The human animal, like all animals, has a well-rehearsed threefold response to threat, it is: fight, flight or freeze. More recently, another has been added: collapse. My response, on this occasion, to whatever I had experienced in the therapy room, was to freeze. Had John pushed me a little too much? Had I experienced challenge without enough support? Whatever had happened, triggered for me an earlier life experience. A series of recollections flooded my mind, starting with the ritual of Sunday dinner, which was a weekly event with us children gathered around the dining table for the typical of-its-time 'meat and two veg' meal. War-time rationing had instilled in my parents a hatred of waste, so we children would have to sit there until everything on our plates was eaten. No concessions were made towards a hatred of sprouts or a dislike of runner beans. But this is not the lingering or depressing memory.

These times were not convivial occasions of sharing news as well as food. They were silent sullen times, interspersed with sergeant-major like commands such as:

'Don't speak until you're spoken to.'

'Don't speak out of turn.'

'Sit up straight, get your arms off the table.'

'Don't speak with your mouth full.'

This last statement being somewhat redundant given that we had already been told not to speak. We were children, these orders were frequently disobeyed, and transgression resulted in being shouted at, sworn at and, not infrequently, hit around the head. Strangely, when my father had been out for a pre-dinner visit to the pub, he was more mellow.

When I was furnishing my own home, this childhood memory of sitting at a square dining table, spurred me on to buy a round dining table. A circular shape meant that when I had a family we would eat together on an equal basis.

Father, mother, sister, brother, friend, lover, they all show up in the therapy room. Transference occurs when memories and qualities of a relationship from the past make their way into the present. Perhaps transference is present in all new relationships, after all we use what we know as the building bricks for creating new connections. We may have an unspoken conversation within assessing the compatibility of this newcomer. Elements of experience will give us the courage to reach out to others and get to know them. Transference can form a bridge for us to cross as we form new relationships and meet the reality of this new 'other'.

In therapy that which is being transferred onto the therapist can be a useful tool for understanding the needs of the client. As I reflected on the session that found me frozen and led to the writing of the poem 'Brain Freeze', I realised something had happened to turn my therapist into my father, to this day I don't know what that was. I perceived some kind of threat resulting in a shut down and withdrawal. My therapist was no longer John, the person I knew well, he became for me a hostile threat. I knew cognitively that he was working hard towards my healing, for many months I had experienced him as a person of immense kindness and patience, but in the moments of my frozenness, I lost all sense of that. Hence the lines:

And I know you are not my father

I know your desire is to heal not harm.

But in those moments, minutes, hours of 'brain freeze'

I forget and cannot access your tenderness

it is deleted or rendered 'junk mail'.

Transference can be both help and hindrance. There were times in our sessions when I would become aware of John speaking with a warm and encouraging voice, there would be a motherly or nurturing quality to what was being offered. On one occasion, I was seeing John the day after a quite unpleasant hospital procedure, and as I related the experience to him, I cried like a child with a caring mother. I wept as I told him how it felt, how it hurt me physically when it wasn't expected to, and he listened, attentively, caringly. We both knew that this experience didn't need analysis, it needed honouring and tender listening. I needed to know that I was cared for, not just because I was a client with a therapist. It was because of this quality of caring that healing became possible.

Transference can be a useful tool in the therapeutic process as well as being a heavy burden to bear for the therapist. The aim, however, is to move beyond the transference to the real relationship between two people who meet each other authentically.

Chapter Thirteen

PARISH MATTERS

My area Bishop called me in for a meeting, I had been in post in my new parishes for just over twelve months and we were at the point of making my role permanent. My tenure as priest-in-charge was coming to an end, I was going to be installed as vicar. He began, 'You will have learned by now that your parishes don't have a history of being kind to their clergy.' I thought, 'Thanks, Bishop. Why didn't you tell me that a year ago? I might have reconsidered accepting the post?' At least, I wouldn't have spent twelve months wondering what I was doing wrong and thinking it was all my fault. The Bishop was right; I had learned to my cost that my new parishes had a diocesan-wide reputation for being 'difficult'. A handful of parishioners had made it their mission to write to the senior staff, including the Bishop, on a regular basis, to complain about the shortcomings of the current incumbent.

These rural parishes were set in a beautiful location, the church buildings were magnificent yet like many congregations, renewal was needed. Fresh ideas and new vision were needed to help them to become outward looking and more able to reach out to the local community. There is a truth in life that growth requires change and if growth isn't happening in an institution, it is slowly dying. The church is no exception to this. As the new minister, I was keen to look for the potential for growth. I have always tried to ask a church to consider what we would look like to a complete outsider or occasional visitor. Would the average non-churchgoer find a welcome among us? Should they take the risk of showing up one Sunday? I was keen to inject some new life into the worshipping life of these fairly trad churches. So, early on, I introduced my guitar. Attempting to bring some fun and liveliness in our services for the sake of those who were young in years as well as heart, I would lead one of the newer worship songs. Most people enjoyed my style, a powerful minority did not and would write to the Bishop regularly complaining about me. The man championing the appeal to raise funds to refurbish the organ never missed an opportunity to complain to anyone who would listen that I took no interest in his work, and that I was being neglectful of my duties. He would regularly ambush me after I had just led the morning service to regale me with his concerns, oblivious to the fact that I was trying to engage some of the younger families who had dared to join us.

On one occasion, I simply said to him, when he accused me yet again of not doing my job properly: 'You don't need a priest to fund raise for the new organ, that is not what a priest is for.' If he had been a lone voice, I could have coped, but there were others. Some of the people who complained about me never came to Sunday worship but positioned themselves on the church council. This small minority took every opportunity to complain, a group which would eventually drive us out.

What I was learning in therapy, during this time, about transference and holding one's psychological boundaries, was invaluable. The role of the clergyperson, especially a vicar, is a lonely one. As vicar I was leader of two Christian communities who looked to me for guidance, inspiration and pastoral care. My heart has always been for the ones who are seeking faith and meaning in life, the ones who need to come to church but don't because they think they are not good enough or will not be welcome. It is all too easy for long-term members of a church to feel neglected when the vicar pays attention to the newcomer, unless they share the opinion of William Temple, former Archbishop of Canterbury (1942–4) that:

The Church is the only organisation
   that does not exist for itself,
      but for those who live outside of it.

One August, I returned from holiday to be told of an elderly church member who had not attended church for several weeks because of illness, so I went to visit him. Did he greet me with the words 'thank you for coming'? No, he told me quite bluntly, in as many words, that I was not suited to be a vicar as I hadn't come to see him sooner. Was he interested in the fact that I had only just learned of his situation, or that I had been away? He was not. His words to me were: 'You may be suitable for something, Charmaine, but not a vicar.'

Those words broke me inside. Yet, I had to maintain a polite pastoral presence with him and carry on in my role as vicar with his pronouncement searing my soul. Later that day, I was angry, livid at the injustice of his judgement. I wanted to revisit and retaliate, defend myself and use four-letter words to tell him what he could do with himself.

Like many church leaders, I was wide open to be the recipient of transference and projection. It begins as people start to realise I am not the compassionate mother they have always been searching for. It continues when I am experienced as the persecuting parent because I don't or can't comply with their wishes. I am me, trying to do the best I can. I have often wished that churches would celebrate the priest they do have rather than lament the one they don't. Couldn't my churches see what I was bringing to them and rejoice rather than constantly look for what was missing? I would tell them often that if they were looking for faults, they would easily find them, I was more aware than anyone of my shortcomings. Imposter syndrome was a constant companion.

Hardest of all, was when people who I thought were allies or shared my vision turned on me, though I doubt that they would see it like that. One day, I received a letter in the post from two people I thought were friends. In it they expressed disappointment with me over some perceived slight they felt. They also informed me that they had consulted with the Archdeacon querying the validity of an action I had taken. I don't remember what the actual complaint was, but I felt an acute sense of betrayal that people I trusted would do this. One of them had my mobile phone number, was a Facebook friend and regularly texted me. Why would he resort to sending a formal letter of complaint to me?

I was overwhelmed with shame, and wondered again what had gone wrong, how had I been so misunderstood? What had I missed?

It was the invocation of the Archdeacon that triggered my own transference response. A crushing shame is evoked within me whenever I hear that someone has 'written to the Archdeacon'. Even an email from an Archdeacon's personal assistant causes me to freeze for a moment. Why would this be? Does everyone have this response to authority figures?

The problem for church life is that there are two dynamics in play. The first is that we are all equal in Christ, something that is declared in scripture. In the New Testament letter of Paul to the Galatians, chapter 3:28, spells it out:

There is neither Jew nor Gentile, neither slave nor free, nor is there male and female, for you are all one in Christ Jesus.

New International Version

Then, again, in the gospel of John, chapter 15:15, we have the words of Jesus:

I no longer call you servants because a servant does not know his master's business. Instead, I have called you friends, for everything that I learned from my Father I have made known to you.

New International Version

The second is this: parish priests are to serve their people with love, but they are also caught up in a hierarchy of Bishops and Archdeacons. These days, there are regular appraisals and a disciplinary process, and though it could be that most senior staff would like to see themselves as supportive and caring, they, too, are caught up in a system of power dynamics. The vocation is to love the people whilst being in a very vulnerable and isolated position. This means that I was open to criticism from those same people and at the same time answerable to the institutional superiors.

There is another side to parochial life. There are many times of joy and fun. One memorable time was the wedding of Prince William to Katherine Middleton. Some months prior to this, a group of women approached me to ask if I would be willing to allow them to organise a wedding event in the parish church. They wanted to arrange for the wedding to be shown live on a big screen in the church building with a village-wide invitation going out to everyone. There were to be wedding outfits, prosecco, canapes, photographs and even a wedding cake. Of course, I said yes! A group of people wanting to organise a community event in your church that wouldn't ask anything of you other than turning up is every parish priest's dream!

The day came, I was in my best mother-of-the bride outfit, complete with hat, which hadn't been worn since my own daughter's wedding. People flocked to church to be part of 'the wedding', even the local MP with his young family. To my amazement, as the entrance music began, and Katherine, the bride, entered on her father's arm, the whole gathering stood. We were now part of the congregation attending the royal wedding; we sang the hymns, witnessed the exchange of vows, and listened to the sermon. Afterwards, because I was the vicar, I was invited to cut the cake!

The local primary school also seemed preoccupied with weddings. Every year they would ask to come to the church for a pretend wedding service; to be honest, I was not very keen on this. The village school liked to play host to an inner-city school with the hope that both sets of children would benefit from sharing in this activity. So, two children were asked to be the bride and groom, others were bridesmaids and best men, the rest of the children were the congregation. It was surreal going through the marriage service with these infant children while making it clear to everyone there that it was only pretend. This boy and girl were not joined for better or worse and for life.

When it was all over, everyone would return to the school for the reception. Children from both schools met up for a shared lunch, and because none of the pupils from the visiting school knew me, I mingled among them to say hello.

One girl looked at me with curiosity trying to place me. She had seen me in church, fully robed conducting the wedding ceremony, but was unsure if I was the same person. Her next question stopped me in my tracks. With wide innocent eyes she asked, 'Are you the Pope?'

I cannot tell you how tempted I was to answer in the affirmative.

From the ridiculous to the sublime, there were also times of great privilege with my role as parish priest. There would be the meeting with a couple arranging a baptism for their much-wanted baby, hearing their story of enduring several rounds of IVF before, finally, the safe arrival of their child.

No wonder they wanted to give thanks.

Chapter Fourteen

POETRY, PICTURES AND PRAYER

Two years into my therapy and the going got tough. By this point, I had completed the formal part of my own counsellor training, so continuing to see a therapist was optional rather than a course requirement. I thought I would have to stop seeing John and that maybe he would no longer be interested in working with me. This was distressing. When I told him he responded in typical fashion: 'Charmaine, the work has only just started, anyone looking in from the outside would say that we are only two years into a five-year piece of work. This is where the work becomes creative now!'

He was right, it did become creative.

The therapeutic alliance was solid, the relationship secure enough to face and work through the psychological pain I carried within me. We would continue to have our weekly one-hour sessions and I would return home and weep. It was counter-intuitive to me that the sessions, which seemed so good and connecting, would result this way. I was learning that psychotherapy, healing of the soul, did not just happen during the hour I met with my therapist, but continued through the rest of life. It was not like a tap was switched on for an hour and then was turned off until the following week, it was more like a water source was being unblocked and would flow freely until we met again.

I kept a regular journal. I made notes on the session, I wrote down how I felt and, most importantly, I recorded my dreams. Dreaming was frequent and the dreams vivid, and many of our sessions involved exploring their content. What was I trying to tell myself in the dreams? What breakthrough might there be in psychological understanding?

And I wrote poetry. I had never written poetry in my life before, seriously, never. But now, it was as though regular narrative description couldn't do justice to the emotions I wanted to express; the poems were like a code. It was as though there were some things I wanted to communicate, that I dare not voice, except in poetic form. Years later in therapy, when I was working through issues at a very cognitive, adult-to-adult level, I realised that most of the subjects that came up had been expressed much earlier in my poetry. The poems were like the child voice in me wanting to be heard but not fully under-standing how to find the right words or even what the subject was. The poems would not stop coming, the words poured out, ready assembled onto the page.

I am an articulate person. I express myself well. I also speak French with a measure of fluency, thanks to my year as an au pair in Switzerland. But the language of intimacy was new. I had to learn it.

In the gospel of John, chapter 4, Jesus meets a Samaritan woman at a well in the middle of the day. He asks her for a drink of water. There are many taboos about this meeting, not least that she is a woman, alone in broad daylight, conversing with a man. She is a Samaritan encountering a Jew, they are from different people groups, hostile to each other. He approaches her and asks for a drink. She replies, 'You are a Jew, and I am a Samaritan woman. How can you ask me for a drink?' Jesus replies something to the effect: 'If only you knew who you're talking to'. There follows a fair bit of banter between the two of them, then the conversation deepens, as he identifies the ache in her heart brought about by a series of failed relationships. This is a deeply intimate encounter. As they share their stories, the human need for connection is met and both lives are changed by the meeting. It is a good image of a therapeutic engagement.

Alongside writing poetry, I also began to make pictures. Art therapy is its own discipline, and though I was not a trained art therapist, I had learned about using art materials with a client in my own Gestalt therapeutic training. As would-be counsellors, we had great fun using pastels and exploring mark making to create visual images; specifically, we created mandalas.

Mandalas are circular designs that reflect the wholeness of the person creating them. The Swiss psychiatrist, Carl Jung, described a mandala as the psychological expression of the totality of the self. He discovered their significance through his own inner work.

Likewise, for my own work, when words failed or escaped me, putting pastel to paper, I could create images, typically starting with a circle. I would then see what colours attracted me and enjoy the tactile sensation of moving pastel crayons across the paper. Using the flats of both hands I created patterns and shapes to express my inner turmoil. Moving rhythmically and bodily, facilitated in me a sense of calm and resolution. The pictures I created would join me on my journey to see John, and I would often arrive at my therapy session bearing a portfolio of pictures that we would look at together. Later, when I applied to the Adult Education Service to do a course in Art and Design, I had to take some artwork to my interview. The only artwork I had ever done were these abstract pastels. It felt quite odd showing the art tutor images that only John, as my therapist, had seen! Equally interesting, were the tutor's reflections on them as he read them with an artist's eye.

It raised a question for me; Is there a difference between art that is made for therapeutic reasons and art that is created for public viewing? When I turned to my paper and pastels as part of my healing process, I was not for a moment considering what the outcome looked like. It was an exercise in expressing my heart, my soul, bypassing a cognitive filter. Consequently, it felt exposing to have a professional art educator regard them. Nevertheless his comments were revealing.

One picture, which I called 'Jonah Day 4' was an abstract portrayal of the story from the Old Testament, Jonah and the whale. Jonah was being thrown overboard with the whale lying in wait to consume him. I explained that this image expressed how I felt one time, like I was drowning. The tutor paused for a moment then replied, 'Did you get to Nineveh?' I was taken by surprise and thought to myself, 'Does this man have inside knowledge?' I learned later that he indeed did. He had once been a Sunday School teacher!

The second picture I showed the tutor depicted short diagonal lines in different colours with a swirl of colour in the top right-hand corner. The tutor observed that this image looked as though something was trying to get away, but it had become trapped. He was spot on, but I had not seen it before that moment.

There was a freedom in working this way. In earlier years, my attempts at art, even in primary school, had been met with criticism and derision. The memory still stings of a time when, at the tender age of six, I was doing my best to colour in a picture of Jesus and I was roundly told off for not 'keeping within the lines', and what a mess I was making of it. Perhaps art is taught with more encouragement these days.

'Keeping within the lines' is also a psychological constriction, something imposed on the human spirit, perhaps especially so on women. My work these days is to keep trying to move beyond the lines and extend my boundaries.

I needed to express myself this way, and have another person look at the images with me. Making art this way gave me a wonderful sense of play, this, too, was a new experience.

I now had 'poetry' and 'pictures', but what happened to 'prayer'?

At my first session with John, he told me he wouldn't pray for me in the session. This was because a power imbalance in favour of the therapist, was already there, and prayer only added to that. I was relieved. We are both people of prayer, and it could be said of clergy that we are paid to pray. So why not now in a therapy session?

There are two schools of thought about the place of prayer in the counselling room. The first is that it is inappropriate because of the potential for the therapist to exercise undue power over, or manipulate, the client. It can also be used as a way of avoiding issues, hiding behind a sense of piety rather than face challenging issues. An alternative view is that it can be helpful in the therapy room, especially if the client uses prayer as a resource for themselves. The therapist, too, might believe that prayer is an important and valid therapeutic tool, which, if used with care, can be helpful to the client.

My own practice as a counsellor was not to offer prayer in the session, though I did hold my clients prayerfully in my heart before meeting with them, and many times, after the session, as I thought about what they were dealing with in life. The people who met with me at the counselling agency where I volunteered, usually didn't know I was a clergywoman or even a person of faith. Though, sometimes, a client would request to meet with a counsellor who was a Christian. There were two occasions when, at the end of the session, I was asked to pray for my clients to conclude the session. Although I would not have offered to pray, it was clear to me that for the client it was important that I did pray. An interesting exercise would have been to explore the reasons why it was important, but that was not the task in hand. And, as always in counselling, both therapist and client must choose the pathways to go down and in so doing, leave the others untravelled, at least for a while.

As parish priests, John and I were both used to praying with people, even using touch by laying a hand on an arm or a shoulder of an individual, with their permission, to reassure them. This did not become part of our therapeutic meetings. Neither, for a long time, did any mention of God occur. We had already identified that authority figures were problematic for me, and there is no greater authority figure than God! I was learning to reclaim my own power, so it was important to have the freedom to dispense with all authority figures during this process. This was exquisitely liberating, I was paid to be a professional Christian, it felt subversive to flirt with atheism! Although, even this led me to a new understanding of God.

One day, I had a fresh realisation, even an epiphany, that If

God is God, then he didn't depend on me to believe in him for his existence, and if he isn't God, it doesn't matter. For all my professional life as a Christian minister, I have been aware of other people's faith depending on me. I am, quite reasonably, expected to believe in Christianity, to practice what I preach. But what if, for a season, I could lay this down? Could I take the risk of the uncertainty of not knowing? The result of this question was that I went through a period when I didn't know what to preach about anymore. What could I say from the pulpit with integrity? I spoke about love. This therapeutic pilgrimage was a journey of love. It was about learning first how to love myself. So even though John and I didn't pray when we met together, I know there was a great deal of prayer on both our parts before and afterwards. And, while God was rarely named, the presence of a third divine presence in the therapy room was, at times, almost tangible.

This sense of spiritual presence would sometimes occur as silence fell between the two of us, when, without speech, there was profound communication – a wordless intimacy. It is a powerful thing to be held in the gaze of another. How often in everyday life do we really look at one another, see each other's faces? Generally, we don't. I had been raised on a diet of 'it's rude to stare' but take the average two-year-old and they will stare until they have taken in all the information they want from the object of their gaze. If they are fortunate, they will have loving caregivers who lavish a loving gaze upon them from birth. The reason many of us end up in therapy is because we are fed up with hiding from the world, from ourselves and we want to learn who we really are. We want to be seen; we crave a loving gaze. That was the reason I was there.

Chapter Fifteen

LABYRINTHS AND BROKEN ROADS

An ordained person in the Church of England can apply for a sabbatical every few years. A sabbatical is a period when you can take time off and be relieved of parochial duties. Quality time is needed to tend to your own soul when you are tasked with the 'cure of souls'. A sabbatical of three months is permitted after seven years in the same parish.

I had been four years in my current role as vicar and desperately needed a sabbatical. The challenges and criticism were grinding me down, so without too much hope, I applied for a period of leave for 2014. It didn't help that I was new to this diocese, and though my last sabbatical in France had been more than ten years earlier I was not optimistic. To my amazement and delight, I was granted a sabbatical. I wondered if it was because senior staff took pity on me and wanted me to have a respite from the constant complaining of the vocal few or perhaps because they wanted a break from the same. I expressed my delight and surprise to the officer who allocated sabbaticals only to be told that I had made the cut because applications were low that year!

A sabbatical is sometimes called study leave, and I had been granted one! A cynical person might suggest that the second of those titles was invented to satisfy the workaholics and grant-making bodies. Taking time out to travel, for whatever reason, is costly, and there are organisations that award grants to clergy for sabbatical leave. It always looks better on the application to say that you want funds to help you do something that will benefit humankind, or at least your own parishioners. There are some people who can't countenance that it's ok to just have quality time off to recharge the batteries. Or it may be that as clergy we are aware of the privilege of being in a line of work that allows the luxury of three months paid leave. I understand that, so, could I justify it?

By this time I had lived in a vicarage for more than twenty years. It was quite a luxury to live in a large, detached, four-bedroomed house, the likes of which I will never be able to afford. But my house didn't belong to me, I didn't own it. Like many vicarages, as well as providing a home for me and my family, it also served as my office, the parish office, the meeting room, the hospitality suite and is available to anyone who wants to call in. My working week was a six-day week with one day off and every weekend on duty; making it very difficult to be off duty at home. And thanks to the ubiquity of smart phones, and the lack of discipline of their owners, emails are constantly checked, and phone calls answered. The working day does not end, conveniently at 5.30pm when the troubles and joys of the day can be left behind, that only happens when away from the home, on holiday, or on sabbatical. A clergyperson is the one remaining professional who lives at the centre of where they work.

The trouble with being given permission for a three-month sabbatical is that you must decide what to do with it. Some clergy don't even bother to apply for a sabbatical because the headache of deciding where to go and what to do is almost as stressful as carrying on without one. Decisions about where to go, and the attendant cost can often hinder. But to stay at home, is not an option if a complete break is needed. I was fortunate in that I no longer needed to plan around school terms and Ian's career, he was already retired. And as our eldest daughter lived in the United States with twin baby girls, a visit to her needed to be included. Thankfully, I had John to talk this over with.

One gloomy Thursday afternoon as I lamented that I couldn't decide what to do, John asked, 'What are your options?'. 'Well,' I began, 'I could work for my masters in pastoral counselling and use the time to write up my dissertation.' I was now a qualified counsellor and there was the opportunity to go on to study for a master's degree. This felt a worthy choice, it would justify the use of time off from parish commitments. John listened for a moment and then asked, 'Ok, what do you really want to do?' Without a moment's hesitation I declared, 'I want to go to Nashville.' With a response that was worthy of textbook therapy, he replied, 'There was a lot more energy about that statement.' It was true, I really did want to go to Nashville, but why?

This therapeutic journey I was on was enabling me to flourish and realise my creative gifts. I had already begun to paint and write poetry; I had also fallen in love with country music. In my parish there was a folk club, and one Thursday evening I had gone along to listen to the performers. They had welcomed me with open arms and when they had learned that I was the local vicar the word had gone around, 'Mind your language, the parson's here!' Of course, they never did mind their language. I became a regular and with their encouragement, I started playing my guitar again and as a performer, I came alive.

Brewood folk club was like a church for me. They were an appreciative audience whenever I sang from my limited repertoire and thanks to their encouragement, my confidence grew. It was not actually a church, and as far as I knew, none of the members were church goers, but there was an extraordinary level of pastoral care among them. Sometimes there was an almost palpable sense of divine presence as people sang from the heart.

As I could never quite remember the words and chords of the song I was about to sing, I had them in front of me on a music stand. One night the resident host, in his thick black country accent, said, 'Yow'm much better when yow're not looking down at yer words!' It got me thinking, 'Did I know any songs that I didn't need the words for?' I wracked my brains. I knew plenty of hymns off by heart. So, I double checked that I did know all the words to the song I was about to sing, I announced that I was going to sing a song from my day job. I introduced the song as a number one hit from the 1960s and began to sing Amazing Grace. Every single person present joined in. It was a holy moment.

But could I really take the risk of going right outside of my comfort zone and travel to Nashville? And if I went there, what would I do? I knew I wanted to be more than just one more devotee who travels to Music City as a tourist. You can be a tourist anywhere in the world, I wanted to know what it was like being part of a community in Nashville. But again, why Nashville?

Many months before, as I prepared to go away on a five-day retreat, I emptied long forgotten jacket pockets and suitcases. To my surprise, I came across a small scrap of paper with the words 'Bless the Broken Road' written on it. At first, I thought it might be something my daughter had given to me, but the handwriting was clearly mine. I was intrigued, curious, I had no recollection of writing it, neither did I know to what it referred. What on earth was this hidden message in my pocket? There was only one thing to do, I googled it. My internet search led me to a song by the country music band, Rascal Flatts. The song is 'Bless the Broken Road' and the words spoke deeply to my soul. This was the start of my love affair with country music.

Discovering this note could not have been more portentous. The retreat I had booked was a labyrinth retreat. The most famous labyrinth is at Chartres Cathedral in France, where for decades people have walked the circular pattern as a way of making a pilgrimage. The design invites a rhythmical pattern of walking which centres the mind and enables meditation. I had been intrigued by labyrinthine patterns for some time and was excited to be going on this retreat to learn more.

When you walk a labyrinth, you follow the path that leads to the centre, though on first sight it is not obvious how to get to there. It is a walk of trust. As you follow the path step by step, it can seem as though you are being taken further away from the centre, but if you keep going and trust the pathway, all at once you find you have arrived. Unlike a maze, where you can get lost, a labyrinth is designed to help you find your way.

The song, 'Bless the Broken Road' was a perfect fit for the start of a labyrinth retreat. Not just that, but both the labyrinth and the song formed a narrative for this stage of my life. Where was my life going? What about the wrong turns I had taken, the dead ends? Could they still be part of my finding my way forward?

So, Nashville would form at least part of my sabbatical leave. The question was: how?

Another element of this sabbatical would be some time spent solo, on my own without Ian. Already my therapeutic journey had had me facing questions about who I was when I wasn't someone's wife, mother, daughter, sister or vicar. Now, it was time to find this out in the big wide world by placing myself in a context where only I would be known. I would go out and meet people without the security blanket of an attentive spouse. This idea appealed to me; I was quite excited about it. Not that I wanted to be single or without a family, but I did want to test my own boundaries and be in touch with my own resources. Fortunately, because my daughter was living in the USA and her twin girls were only a few months old, I knew that she would welcome the support of her father during the time that I would be occupied with my Nashville project. I was equally daunted by the prospect of a three-month period without therapy; something would have to be done about that. But first things first, how was I going to set up my Nashville adventure?

Just as the song 'Bless the Broken Road' came to me, almost by divine appointment, so did the next step of the journey. One day, at a meeting of local clergy, I wanted to go public with my plan to spend some time in Nashville for my upcoming sabbatical. I shared with colleagues my plane to travel to the heart of country music, because of the discovery of that music and the song 'Bless the Broken Road'. There was a pause in the room, and I wondered if they were thinking, 'Typical, another of Charmaine's hare-brained schemes'. I could imagine their unspoken questions asking, 'What's that got to do with parish ministry?' I was asking those questions myself until someone said: 'I heard a woman speak at Greenbelt [the annual Christian Arts Festival], it was her husband who wrote that song. She is a woman priest in Nashville, and her husband sang that song as part of her presentation.'

Still, to this day I can hardly believe how events unfolded like this. I find a song that makes me want to go to Nashville, and then, randomly, I discover that a neighbouring vicar has heard it sung by the man who wrote it. Now I had a contact in Nashville, the Episcopalian priest Reverend Becca Stevens. The next thing was to write to her. But what should I write? It didn't feel enough to declare that I wanted to come to Nashville and could she help. So, I decided to write and introduce myself as a priest in the Church of England and mention that I was a folk singer who had found my local folk group to be a source of spiritual support and encouragement. I told her that I had come across her husband's song at a significant time in my life which led me wanting to explore the spirituality of country music in its natural homeland. I sent the letter. To my astonishment, Becca replied with, 'Come, you will be welcome.'

Chapter Sixteen

CALIFORNIA DREAMING

'Come, you will be welcome.'
Yes, but how? There wasn't a magic carpet ride that would transport me safely to ready-made accommodation. I still had to make many arrangements. And what if this American priest had expectations of me that I couldn't deliver? The euphoric high of finding a contact in Nashville, rapidly gave way to the opposite: deep and dark anxiety. Suddenly, I wanted to call it all off. I said as much the next time I saw John.

He listened with patience as I began to backtrack on my decision about Nashville, though I suspect underneath there may have been a measure of frustration on his part with this oscillating client. I began with, 'Perhaps Nashville is just a metaphor for moving forward psychologically. Maybe I don't have to go to Nashville, it's just representing something else from my unconscious processes.' By this point in therapy, I was becoming quite skilled at my own analysis, even to the point of noticing when I was using psychological speak as a defence against my fears. The truth was, I was now terrified by the prospect of having to realise a dream and bring it to birth. I would have given anything, everything, for John to reply, 'Of course you don't have to go, in fact you shouldn't, stay here with me where it's safe.' But he didn't. With a voice so low I could barely hear him, a technique he often used when trying to get me to focus, the unexpected reply came: 'Charmaine, no, you don't have to go to Nashville, but if you don't, I think you will regret it 'til your dying day.' I had to go to Nashville. John didn't do soothing.

However, before Nashville, there was California. California was a late inclusion in sabbatical planning when, after a hard day's browsing the internet, I noticed a post on social media advertising a retreat for leaders, led by a favourite Christian teacher of mine. The American pastor and writer, Rob Bell, was holding a two-day retreat in Laguna Beach, California. Reading his books and blog posts had been part of my recovery, not least of my Christian faith. I had already thought idly about how good it would be to sit at his feet and learn first-hand from this American pastor. All I knew of him was that he was a successful leader of a mega church in the United States who attracted controversy because of his best-selling book *Love Wins*. I imagined that if by some amazing chance I could get to see him, I would be one amongst thousands attending a service he was leading. Now here was a chance to realise another dream.

The retreats would be happening in January and February, my sabbatical was due to start in January and Nashville was already booked for March. It was November and although I had not yet booked flights, I knew I couldn't make the January date. Might there be another retreat, a later date towards the end of my sabbatical? I enquired. No, there was not another date but there were still a few spots open on the ones already planned. Could I take the plunge again into the unknown and sign up for one of these? I was helped in this decision, not by my trusty therapist, but by a money back guarantee should I have to cancel within two weeks of the event. Now, in my experience this is almost unheard of when booking for Christian conferences and retreats. This was the safety net I needed. I went to bed planning to book a place the following morning. However, I couldn't wait, what if it was full by tomorrow? California is eight hours behind London so there were still plenty of working hours of time for people to fill up those few remaining places. The result was, following a brief conversation with Ian, promising I would explain it all later, that I booked for the two-day retreat in February 2014 with Rob Bell in Laguna Beach, California.

I would adjust my sabbatical plans. The timetable would now begin with a visit to California, taking in the Leader's Retreat in February. This turned out to be a blessing; not only would I have the month of January to recover from Christmas, an annual necessity for most clergy, there would be more time to prepare for three months away in the United States.

The feast of Candlemas, 2nd February 2014, was my last Sunday on duty until the beginning of May. I danced down the aisle. We left on the next day.

We flew from Manchester airport to San Francisco, with a stopover at Atlanta airport. The seven-hour flight to Atlanta was long enough, but I hadn't grasped that the flight from Atlanta to San Francisco would be almost as long again. Over the years, there had been many visits to our daughter who lived in Alabama. We were quite familiar with the east and south of the United States but now we were headed west. Eventually, we landed in the city of the Golden Gate Bridge thankful to find out hotel next to Pier 39.

The next morning, I woke at 5.30am local time, but my body clock was at 2pm, so it was time to find food. I was starving. The beauty of a visit to the US is that you can find places to eat twenty-four hours a day, seven days a week, and sure enough there was a pancake house just a few doors away waiting to serve us breakfast. Pier 39 is a place full of bustle; it brims with people and restaurants. But in the early hours of this particular Tuesday morning, it was eerily quiet, and spacious enough for a good view of the sea lions reclining on their overnight landings, untroubled by the tourist boats making their way to Alcatraz Island. By 9am, it was important I was back in the hotel room I had a therapy session booked.

In the build up to leaving for my sabbatical, John and I had discussed how we would manage with a three-month break. I felt I wouldn't cope despite his repeated assertions that it was only twelve weeks, and I would be fine. In the end, and as a concession to my growing anxiety about the upcoming expedition, he agreed that we would do our best to keep up our weekly sessions via Skype.

My histrionic tendencies were well known to us both by now and John would sometimes greet my fears about the upcoming travel with a wry smile. He would remind me that I wasn't travelling into the unknown; I was still comfortably placed within the western world where countless tourists have gone before. I also knew from my own experience that on the whole Brits in the US are well liked. But a continuing fear for me was that of abandonment, that I would be forgotten in my absence, and John also knew this well enough to want to offer continuing support.

So, at 9am Californian time and 3pm UK time, we had the

first of my sabbatical Skype sessions. I relaxed; it would be ok. My weekly therapy sessions on Skype would hold me and give me a place to reflect on the new experiences that lay ahead.

The stay in San Francisco was all too brief. There is much more to do and see there than ride the trolley bus, cross the Golden Gate Bridge, and eat lobster at Pier 39. There is also Grace Cathedral to visit with its Chartres-styled labyrinth to walk. I had learned about Grace Cathedral during my labyrinth retreat many months earlier, so it was fitting to begin my sabbatical journey and walk the labyrinth inside Grace Cathedral.

It was a beautiful experience, made even more so by an art installation of multi-coloured ribbons hanging from the vaulted ceiling. Just as walking the labyrinth is a journey of discovery, so was the journey I was about to begin. I knew there were some fixed points planned but I didn't know for sure what lay ahead or the people I would meet.

On the way back to the hotel, we took a detour through the Chinese quarter. The Chinese quarter, now there's a revelation! I asked myself: are we still in the US? With its shops and signage as far as the eye could see it felt like we were, in fact, in China. It was quite disorienting. I had visited the US many times before, but the Chinese quarter was nothing like the US I had come to know; this was indeed China. I was lured into a store selling Chinese style clothing, so as a souvenir of this heady experience I bought a purple and gold dressing gown. Purple and gold, the colours of my healing.

Chapter Seventeen

SURFING USA

Soon it was time to leave San Francisco and head south towards Laguna Beach. Along the way, we discovered the coastal road, the Big Sur. I have never been a great planner when it comes to travel. I hesitate to read the travel guides because they fill me with an anxiety that I will never have time to do justice to all there is to see. So, although I knew where we were headed and where we had hotel reservations, we were going to freestyle along the way making good use of the internet to find and book accommodation on the go.

It was at one budget hotel that we asked which was the best way out of town to head south. The reply came, as though we would already know this: 'You make your way along the Big Sur towards San Simeon.' Thank goodness for that advice. The Big Sur is an awe-inspiring highway hemming the vast Pacific Ocean. It is rugged, rocky, edgy and prone to landslides, which occasionally renders it impassable. Along the way, there are retreat centres. Monastic and new age communities have found it an excellent location for anyone looking to 'drop in and drop out' for a while. Fritz Perls, the guru of my own counselling discipline, Gestalt, made his home along the Big Sur and developed his ideas at the Esalen Centre.

I discovered two more things, thanks to this period of nomadic existence. The first being that Spanish is a common language in California, for many people it is their mother tongue. I became aware of this several times when talking to hotel room maids who couldn't understand me when I spoke in English. Of course, that was also a problem sometimes in the US when just speaking with an English accent. I will always remember the panic I felt when I was in a restaurant struggling to communicate to a waiter that I wanted some water. After he had failed to understand me three times I resorted to my limited use of Spanish and said 'agua?' 'Oh', he said, 'you want water!'

The second discovery turned out to be an absolute delight. On the beach at San Simeon resides a colony of elephant seals, the like of which is usually only seen in a David Attenborough documentary. There they were in full, flabby, hollering presence. They were fascinating; we were mesmerised, but the added delight happened when I discovered the volunteer steward on duty was another Charmaine. There are not many Charmaines in the world; in my lifetime I have met fewer than a dozen. We became instant friends.

There were many signs along the way of a guiding hand leading, and meeting another, rare, 'Charmaine' was just one of them.

Eventually after many more miles travelled, with Ian as an admirable chauffeur, we arrived at Laguna Beach for the two-day retreat with Rob Bell, the first of my major sabbatical plans. We made ourselves comfortable in one of the hotels booked by the travel agent. This was not of the budget variety; it was more of a 'make the most of your vacation in California' class. I wanted to be ready for an early start the following day, so we took an evening stroll to locate the venue. We walked along the beach front searching for a huge American style auditorium. This event was with best-selling author Rob Bell, he had led a congregation of thousands of people. What I found was a small boutique hotel besides the beach with an open-air meeting room designed to fit about one hundred guests. The intimacy of the venue stunned me.

Next morning, kindly escorted by Ian, I arrived to take my place. Rob Bell, this controversial pastor I admired, sat barely an arm's length away from me. As he began to teach, it felt like he was speaking directly to me. He shared his own experience of church leadership and the pressures of that role, he understood what it was like to give your heart and soul to a vocation that left you so drained that you questioned whether you could carry on. This successful pastor spoke of the psychological pain of being misunderstood and how important it was that we took care of our own souls first when we are in the business of nurturing the souls of others. Rob Bell opened his heart to us, and I could tell that here was someone who had made his own therapeutic journey. He, too, had reflected upon and learned from his own wounding in ministry. I wondered a few times if he had been a client of my own therapist, John, as there were so many recognisable themes!

Rob Bell is an enthusiastic surfer which he included as part of the two-day retreat. We were in California, the surfing capital of the world. I was with a keen surfer. There were several surfing outlets along the beach, so I thought, why not sign up for a two-hour surfing session in the company of Rob Bell? To their credit, the instructors hardly batted an eyelid as this overweight, late fifty-something struggled to get into a wet suit. This was followed by a dry run on the sand demonstrating how we would begin in the crouched position on the surfboard and spring to our feet at the right moment to catch the wave. This was going to be more than a gentle ride on the sea. I realised I had been thinking more lilo than surfboard. Nevertheless, undaunted, I was towed out to sea by a willing surf instructor, who by then had realised it was not going to be safe to leave me alone in the Pacific. The instruction was: crouch and spring up. However, I could barely maintain a collapsed prone position! I watched with envy as younger and more lithe retreatants effortlessly surfed their way to shore whilst I was gently towed by the still patient and uncomplaining instructor. Ian could only watch from the shore, peering anxiously out to sea to check whether I was still alive. It was a fabulous, once-in-a-lifetime experience. Surfing in Southern California in early February, what is not to love about that? While the rest of the US was snowbound and much of the UK was under flood water, here was I in a wetsuit, enjoying Californian warmth, on a leader's retreat.

During my Californian dream we also took in Palm Springs and the Joshua Tree National Park. Palm Springs, the once glamourous playground of the rich and famous, is set in the middle of the desert, an oasis of western hedonism. By contrast, the Joshua Tree National Park is barren in winter and yet still has a hidden beauty as it waits for the rain fall to bring it back to life.

The final destination in California was San Diego, an intriguing city bordering Mexico. Even before we arrived as we travelled through Southern California, I became aware of the Spanish influence and missionary zeal of the Roman Catholic colonisers with their strategically placed mission stations.

San Diego, geographically and politically, is in the hands of the US, but historically it is rooted further south. It was here that we learned about the little-reported war between Mexico and the US which had ended badly for Mexico. Much hitherto Mexican territory was lost to the US government, including the state of Texas and California.

Our seventeen days in California came to an end; the labyrinthine road had moved us on. The next stop would be a brief interlude in Alabama before moving on to Nashville. But where was John, what happened to the weekly therapy sessions? For his own reasons, he had needed a break too, the California pilgrimage would be visited therapeutically later.

Chapter Eighteen

MUSIC CITY

I had arrived. I was in Nashville with Ian. The long drive from Alabama, had led us to this city of hopes and dreams. A brief five-day visit there gave us enough time to take in the tourist sights, like the Grand Ol' Opry and the downtown bars, where plenty of hopeful future stars of country music perform, surviving on tips, and grateful for it because behind them is a line of soloists, duos and bands ready to take their place. Talent and music are everywhere in Nashville. Eventually, the day came when Ian left to return to our daughter in Alabama and left me to continue a month-long solo stay in Nashville, but not before I was deposited on the doorstep of Reverend Becca Stevens.

Becca was the Episcopalian priest who had encouraged me to pursue my dream; she was the one who sensed what she described as my 'siren call' to visit Nashville. I only knew her as the chaplain at Vanderbilt University, married to the song-writer who wrote the song that had moved me so deeply.

I arrived at 7am, she had warned me not to be late as we had a lengthy road trip ahead. Becca was booked to speak at a Lent lunch at a church in Memphis, which was a good five-hour drive from Nashville. I hovered on the doorstep, declining her invitation to come in for a cup of tea, in a polite, 'I don't want to be any trouble', kind of way. This typically British way of behaving confounds Americans. But she had impressed on me not to be late, so this unexpected invitation to stop for tea, confused me. Becca sent her son to the door to bring me into the house while she made tea. The next enquiry was even more baffling, she asked, 'Do you have a camera?' I offered my iPad wondering if she wanted me to keep a photographic record of the journey we were about to set off on. The directions continued: 'Stand there, with the guitars in the background, hold this.' I realised that Becca was about to take a photo of me holding the object she was thrusting into my hands, which was a small brass sculpture of an old-fashioned gramophone player. Until that moment I had thought the song 'Bless the Broken Road' was a little-known song known only to me and a handful of other people. This small figurine was the Grammy that was awarded to her husband at the 42nd Annual Grammy Awards (1999) for Best Country Song.

The moment became even more surreal when, before I knew what was happening, Becca had gone to get her husband out of bed to come and have a photograph taken with me. My immediate thought was 'Oh God, he'll think I'm stalking him.'

The Reverend Becca Stevens is a formidable woman. Her warmth and passion for justice make her a dynamic preacher. Her entrepreneurial flair has given birth to a unique social enterprise that has helped hundreds of women out of a life of prostitution and drug addiction and into recovery and employment, yet she signs herself modestly, as a thistle farmer. Thistles grow in the most inhospitable places, they flourish equally in pavement cracks and country meadows, they are an emblem of resilience and determination, characteristics demonstrated in the women rescued by her movement. With Tennessean charm, Becca has galvanized communities across the United States to join her in a movement centred on the belief that love heals.

Most people who seek out Becca Stevens do so because they want to know more about this Thistle Farm movement. They want to learn about the issues that lead women to become trapped in a life of addiction and how to help them. I had the privilege of accidentally being in the company of this amazing woman. The healing pathway that I was following had led me here. My broken road had somehow converged with the brokenness of others because I had heard a song and had fallen in love, with life.

We arrived in Memphis, and I learned about how the movement began with Becca securing a house to provide a safe home for four women. She would often say that it takes a community failing for a woman to end up on the streets, so it requires a community working together to rescue her. These four women had spent many years on the streets, selling their bodies to feed addictions that were usually the result of childhood abuse and trauma. I heard one of these women share her story. Doris, had been on the streets of Nashville for twenty-five years before she found security in this first home. The medical care, therapy and the invitation to belong to a community, made a pathway for her to find healing. Her testimony moved me, and I complimented Doris on the power and eloquence of the story she had just shared. I was humbled by her reply as she said, 'I still can't go to sleep at night without the light on, but if I need the bathroom in the night when I come back to bed, I can sometimes turn the light off. It's progress, and I'll take all the progress I can.'

That weekend was the start of my month-long sojourn in Nashville. There were plenty more interactions with other members of the Nashville community to come, but on a day-to-day basis I was staying in a single room at the Scarritt Bennett Centre. This conference-come-retreat centre was once a women's theological college. I had made the deliberate choice to spend this month on my own in Nashille. Just as in therapy, it was important that I was able to experience life as authentically as I could as *Charmaine*. I could hardly remember a time when I wasn't someone's wife, mother, daughter, sister or priest, so here I was with no role to hide behind. It was by turn, thrilling, scary, lonely and challenging. Thankfully, there was plenty of southern hospitality and warmth to make it possible. And there was therapy.

As arranged, John and I resumed our commitment to weekly therapeutic sessions, thanks to the wonder of Skype. Zoom had not yet made its appearance in the world. In different time zones and countries, we kept to our regular time of Thursday at 3pm UK time which was 9am in Tennessee, this internalised therapeutic relationship came with me, and I was glad of its company. All the highs and lows of the Nashville experience were recounted via the internet, the familiar tears and fears also made their appearance. Thankfully wi-fi was easy to access. So, located in my single student accommodation, I would perch with my mini-iPad propped up on my knees and Skype John. If I became too expressive or agitated John would remind me to keep still so that he didn't become seasick trying to focus on a screen that was distorting as it tried to follow me! He listened with the warmth I had become used to, though he didn't hesitate to challenge me if he thought I was becoming a bit too sorry for myself. One time, as I lamented that this Nashville dream was all a bad idea, and I felt stupid, lonely, and not sure how I was going to manage a month on my own, he issued an abrupt, though unorthodox therapeutic intervention, he told me to brush my hair, put on make-up and go out and talk to someone. He was right.

Throughout my years as a minister, I have always been rather last minute in preparation, much to the frustration of more than one church organist or churchwarden! I have learned from experience how important it is to have church-wardens and organists who are planners, not least to ensure that something is in place for Sunday worship lest inspiration fail. But I continue to be one of life's 'last minute' people. In this new context, alongside Becca, I was introduced to a whole new level of 'last minute' and inspiration. On one occasion we were already making our way down the aisle to begin the Sunday service, when she turned to me and asked, 'Would you like to celebrate communion this morning?' Thankfully, there was more notice the day she asked if I would like to sing something in the service. I was grateful for the invitation and eagerly said, 'Yes, please.' Though, even then, with only a moment's notice, she asked me to introduce myself to the congregation and explain why I was in Nashville.

'Otherwise,' she added, 'they'll all be wondering why you are trying to sound like Adele'.

Not that for a minute they would mistake my singing for the internationally acclaimed superstar! She meant that they would wonder about my English accent. So, I introduced myself, explaining that I was in Nashville because I had fallen in love with country music when I had heard a little-known song called 'Bless the Broken Road' which made me want to journey to Music City. They laughed. 'Oh, you think I'm joking,' I clarified. 'No, really, I had no idea it was a Grammy award winning classic. Country music in the UK is not what it is in the USA!'

The time came to sing in the service. Becca was preaching about intimacy, so I sang a modern worship song 'Draw Me Close to You'. Sometimes it is good to not know who is in your audience. By the time I had been there a month, I had discovered that the church was knee deep in singer songwriters. I am so glad I sang that first Sunday in blissful ignorance of that fact. I would never have dared to sing and play the guitar in front of them if I'd known otherwise.

I wasn't going to become famous in Nashville as a singer, there are far too many others in pursuit of that dream. After the service, people came up to me to express their appreciation of my song, someone told me a well-known Nashville joke.

'Do you know how to get rid of a singer on your doorstep? You buy him a pizza.' I didn't entirely get this until later, when I learned just how many musicians there are in Nashville trying to make a living on tips.

Nashville itself is a city awash with talented, creative people. It hums with energy. Famous faces and names live, work, shop and dine out in the community, shoulder to shoulder with their neighbours. One time during my stay, there was a rumour that a queen of country music would be giving an open-air concert in aid of pet welfare; she is animal lover. The day arrived and I made my way to the venue with one of my new Nashville friends. Sure enough, in a pet shop car park on a street corner of a Nashville suburb, there she was, Emmylou Harris. On a rainy Saturday morning she sang and played the guitar to an audience of around a dozen. I thought to myself: 'Nashville, you are spoiled, with so much talent on your doorstep you don't even bother to turn out for Emmylou Harris!'

Nashville also boasts the Blair School of Music, a centre of excellence in musical education. The school was celebrating its fiftieth anniversary by offering a season of free concerts. As I walked to the school on one dark and rainy evening, I felt lonely. Not for the first time I wondered why I had made the choice to be on my own in Nashville. Then the thought came: 'You have only one life, embrace this unique experience, it will not come again.'

In Nashville, the opportunity to experience live music is endless. A local free newspaper brims with venues to see artist performances. From the superstars at the Bridgetown Arena in downtown Nashville to the up-and-coming artists performing at small and intimate bars on the outskirts. The famous Blue-bird Café is one such venue. I might have easily missed this shop front among many including a drycleaners and a sand-wich shop if it were not for the long line of people outside. They hope to be lucky enough to knab a ticket for that evening's 'singer-songwriters round'. Once inside, this ordi-nary looking shop transforms into a magical eatery, with servers weaving their way through the tightly packed tables that circle around the performers.

The 'singer-songwriter round' is a Nashville speciality. Four people take it in turn to perform, one after the other. Each artist tells the story that led to the song, and every song is their own original composition. With banter, self-depreciation and plenty of mutual admiration, each performer is supported by their musical buddies. I hear it said that all you need for country music is three chords and the truth; but on most occa-sions I heard much more: loss, longing, love, life and faith. Yes, faith. I had already observed that churchgoing in Nashville was not unusual, neither was it unusual to hear a song lyric that talked about belief in God. A song lyric might describe how God had met the singer-songwriter at their lowest point, or how Jesus had saved them from taking a wrong turn. This often confounds many a British country music fan who can't understand why someone would want or need to include meeting Jesus in the story of their song.

Fame was not going to come my way in Nashville, and that wasn't the purpose of my visit, but something else did find me: a renewal of vocation.

There have been women priests in the Episcopal Church of the United States since the 1970s, twenty years earlier than those of us who were the first in the Church of England in 1994. So, unlike the UK, where there is still opposition and resistance to women priests, even in the church where I was ministering, there is widespread acceptance in the USA of women in church leadership.

It was in this context, as I broke bread and blessed wine for sacramental sharing that I knew this was my vocation, I was meant to be a priest. All the hurt and criticism of recent years had taken its toll, I had lost confidence, lost heart and doubted my calling. Even worse, I thought I was a failure. Thanks to the warmth acceptance and encouragement of Becca Stevens and her congregation, I felt loved. I experienced a new sense of calling. It was as though I had woken from a long sleep. Celebrating Holy Communion in St. Augustine's Chapel, I felt I had come home. The familiar ritual rekindled a sense that this was what I had always been meant to do. Even the confidence to call myself a priest was new. The flavour of churchmanship that shaped me resists the term 'priest' preferring the word minister. The term priest is associated with the Roman Catholic Church, or the wing of the Anglican Church called

'High Church' or Anglo-Catholic. For the first time in twenty-five years of ordained life, I started to describe myself as a priest. Something inside of me was released, it was ok to be who I was, who I am.

Months earlier, in the therapist office, I had been counselled that if I didn't go to Nashville when I had the opportunity, I would regret it to my dying day. Thank God I didn't have to live with that regret. But eventually, the time came to leave. So early one morning, I made my way to the airport to take a Southern Airways flight to join my family on vacation in Panama City, Florida. There were tears, but I left having learned something of the Thistle Farmer's mantra, that 'love heals'.

Chapter Nineteen

RETURNING HOME

Surely no-one can spend time in the company of singer-songwriters without wanting to try their hand at doing the same? So, I wrote a song. The inspiration came from a sermon I had heard at St. Augustine's about the woman who met Jesus at the well. The meeting had been transformative for both the woman and, arguably, for Jesus, too. It made me think about all the people that I had met on this sabbatical journey who had changed my life.

Then there is the importance of naming the song. I was learning for myself the power of naming experiences, and the women who were being helped by the Thistle Farm movement were also finding the courage to face and name their woundedness. Shame thrives in the corridors of secrecy holding its victims as prisoners. The way out of it is to name that which has harmed and hurt. But even more basic than that, is the power of simply hearing one's name spoken with empathy. I remember the first time I heard John say my name. He must have used my name many times before but there was one occasion that I heard my name spoken as though for the first time. Name calling is a cruel and violent assault on the psyche; the childhood rhyme of 'sticks and stones may break my bones, but names will never harm me' is a lie. Conversely, to hear one's name spoken with warmth and gentleness is healing. The women at Thistle Farm, Nashville, were healing because they were receiving care and acceptance. They were named. In honour of those women and my Nashville experience, I wrote a song which I would go on and sing at the local folk club.

It was nearly the end of my three-month sabbatical; there would be just time for a short vacation with my family in Florida before it was time to start preparing for a return to my churches in the UK. As the plane touched down at Panama City airport, I began to wonder how I would even begin to share all that I had experienced. Fortunately, life with nine-month-old twin girls sets the priorities, so for now, my Nashville story would wait untold.

The remaining days of my sabbatical held two more delights. The first was visiting the National Park in Florida. National Parks are a feature of American life, each state seems to have at least one. Falling Waters National Park in Florida is well away from the normal tourist spots. This is a park built around several waterfalls, one pours down in torrents into a deep sink hole. It was mesmerising observing from the viewing platform with the sun shining down onto the water, bringing forth the appearance of a rainbow. The rainbow seemed to be dancing in the cascading water. It felt like the waters of baptism were pouring down, bringing renewal and the hope of new beginnings.

In the biblical narrative, the rainbow is a symbol of hope given to Noah as he navigates the flooded earth. From the imprisonment of his self-built ark, the rainbow spoke to him of a new beginning and the waters were receding. The world had been cleansed, forgiven and Noah would find dry land.

For me this waterfall with its dancing rainbow felt like the waters of baptism pouring down, bringing renewal and the hope of a new beginning for me, too.

Rituals are important, and there was one final ritual to perform to conclude my sabbatical in the United States. My daughter and her family lived in Dothan, Alabama and in the neighbourhood is an Episcopalian Church, The Church of the Nativity. They have an outdoor labyrinth. It was Palm Sunday, the start of Holy Week and it was also a joy to attend church for the Easter Celebrations without responsibility for any of them! On Palm Sunday, we gathered around the labyrinth to begin our procession and began the story of Jesus' ride into Jerusalem. We waved palm branches and sang hosanna in the April sun; it was a relief to make our way into the cool of the sanctuary, out of the Alabaman heat.

My labyrinth retreat had been the launch pad for this American adventure. Its broken road was resumed at Grace Cathedral, San Francisco and led me to Nashville so it was appropriate that another labyrinth would conclude this stage of my journey.

Chapter Twenty

TURNING AND RETURNING

After three months in the United States, I felt quite at home. My confidence had grown as I travelled around from place to place with Ian, I had become used to the excellent restaurant service, the cheerful 'have a nice day' and 'I love your accent'.

But it was time to return, not least because our visitor visas were about to expire, and no-one wants to fall foul of the US Homeland Security and jeopardise future family visits.

Besides, I was ready to meet with John, as my therapist, again in the same physical space rather than cyberspace. The day I arrived at his office for the first time in over three months was a sunny day in May. I was full of excitement, ready to tell my sabbatical tales and John greeted me warmly. I had been away for three months, though in a strange way it felt like I had never been away. Staying in touch via Skype had worked well.

Moving on was to become the theme when I returned home. I didn't know this yet, but first there was a date at St.

Paul's Cathedral to honour as 2014 saw the 20th anniversary of the ordination of women to the priesthood in the Church of England.

The Archbishop of Canterbury was to host a service of celebration in honour of this landmark date. Along with all the other women who were first to be ordained priest, I made my way to Dean's Yard, at Westminster Abbey. From there, we processed through the streets of London to St. Paul's Cathedral. Cars were halted as countless women in clerical collars made the pilgrimage to St. Paul's Cathedral, unimpeded by London traffic. We were slower than expected and the traffic police became increasingly anxious that the time allocated to our pedestrian-only right of way would run out. Perhaps we were slower because already many of the women priests were a good age, but equally likely is that there was something of a school-girl adventure about the occasion as we enjoyed the catching up, the gossip and, frankly, the attention. The early May sun was shining down on us, and we were glad. Old friendships were renewed, and new friendships formed. As I shared my mixed experience of parish ministry with one colleague she said: 'The trouble with you Charmaine, you're like Marmite, people either love you or hate you!'

Eventually we arrived. The white dome of St. Paul's welcomed us, and we hurried to don our liturgical vestments ready to gather round the Archbishop of Canterbury for a photograph on the cathedral steps. He was the sole male, purple-clad figure in the centre of a female sea of white cassocks.

The cathedral was full of people, it was a congregation made up of invited guests and supporters. To everyone's surprise, spontaneous applause erupted as we sashayed our way through the nave towards our designated seats beneath the iconic dome. As I sat there, waiting for the service to start, I thought of other memorable occasions which had taken place under this world-famous and much-televised dome. My mind wondered to that other woman, Diana, Princess of Wales, lost from this world too soon, for whom this space had been a final resting place. Neither could I resist taking a sneaky 'under the dome' picture on my iPad, much to the chagrin of my immediate neighbour who reminded me that we had been specifically instructed not to take photographs. Had we? When? Apparently, it was printed in the service booklet. I've never been one for detail.

The Archbishop spoke warmly of the richness women had brought to the ministry of the Church of England. He also acknowledging the pain and challenge of the road many of us had travelled. It was both a celebratory and reflective service of thanksgiving. Afterwards, it became a catch-up occasion of remembering and reminiscing with friends and colleagues not seen since theological college. Had it turned out how we expected? I asked a friend if, knowing what we knew now, would we do it again, make the same choice. I was doubtful until she said: 'But Charmaine, it wasn't really our choice was it.'

I was reminded that this calling, this vocation, was something beyond myself, bigger than any individual's volition.

This was a good place to conclude the sabbatical journeying, it was time to return to the parishes, which meant it was also time to report back to my Bishop. I told him about my adventures in California, in Nashville and St. Paul's Cathedral. I sensed he was genuinely interested. I assured him that I was well-refreshed and ready to throw myself back into my two parishes. I enthused about my renewal of a sense of vocation. He listened and paused before responding with these words:

'Charmaine, I would be happy for you to stay where you are, but you are older than you look, I checked your details today. If you don't move now, you may not be able to in two years-time and I would hate for you to become ground down again, and it is not going to change in those parishes. But if you were thinking of moving there is another ministry position, I'd like you to consider.'

I was fifty-nine.

Chapter Twenty-One

HOLDING ON

My instinct was to hold on, to grip more tightly, then I remembered Willow, our first cat.

She was born in a neighbour's coal shed, so, though amiable enough, there was always something a little feral about her. She rarely came for petting or to sit on a lap, Willow was nomadic in her comings and goings.

A tabby cat, with a multicoloured coat of mottled browns, yellows and blonde, Willow was a beautiful, dainty, feline creature.

One day, she returned home in a sorry state. She had been injured and late at night we took her to the emergency vet who confirmed that she had been hit by a car. How could he know that? The vet pointed to her claws they were jagged and ripped, her paws were grazed, and he went on to explain that when a cat is hit by a car, their first instinct is to dig their claws in. Their survival method is to hold on to the tarmac; it is futile as a defensive action. I could imagine this poor creature being assaulted with such external force and her only defence being to grip even tighter. For a while, it was touch and go for Willow. But thanks to the vet's skill, she made a full recovery and lived for many more years. Like all cat minders, we didn't own Willow, she simply consented to live with us for as long as we fed and watered her, which turned out to be her whole lifetime.

I thought of her instinct to cling on when it would probably have been of more benefit to simply let go. I recognise that in myself. I also employ defence mechanisms that have long since passed their sell-by date. I know only too well, the tendency to want to go back, to hold on to what was, when it would serve me better to let go. Even now, when life stresses mount, creating internal longings, my instinct is to hold on to the past, gripping on tightly to the tarmac of my road, rather than let go and continue the unfolding, unknown path that lies before me. Sometimes I would lament with John that we had moved on and I would want to go back to an earlier session or experience. John rarely pandered to this. He would remind me that I was looking at some of our early sessions with rose coloured spectacles. I realised that we had different perspectives. I would recall wonderful times of learning to trust in therapy thanks to his skill and care, while for him, it was a case of treading carefully with a client whose trauma could be easily triggered resulting in angry outbursts.

The Bishop took me by surprise with his words, I hadn't seen this coming. My first response was to say, 'No thank you, Bishop, I don't need the drop in income, and it would affect my pension.' The post I was being asked to consider was a half-time post, it would mean a fifty percent pay cut. He asked me not to dismiss it out of hand, and added that there might be something that could be done about the pension. I talked it over with a friend who made the astute observation that perhaps the Bishop was right to point out that it would be increasingly difficult for me to move if I left it any longer. Many churches still prefer their clergy to be in their mid-forties with a spouse and family in residence. I was way past that. But it got me thinking. Did I really want to spend the next five years in parishes that had brought me to the edge?

I spent sleepless nights wondering whether I had it in me to leave and start again somewhere new. It is never easy to leave a parish and move to another, and though the past five years had been a challenge, there had been some good new initiatives that I was reluctant to leave. Alongside that, some precious friendships had formed. The strange nature of being a parish priest is that a change of job involves so much more; a house move is just the start. I didn't relish the idea of going to yet another community of people who would weigh up whether they could trust me with the important moments of their lives. Strangers, who would judge me on my choice of hymns and style of preaching, maybe even people who would no longer attend church because I had been appointed. But before even that, there is the process of announcing the move to an unsuspecting congregation and handling their disappointment and grief at the prospect of one more vicar moving on to pastures new.

Thanks to my therapeutic journey, I am familiar with themes of abandonment and loss; they are issues I've been working on for many years. I knew that for many people in my congregations, my leaving would stir up in them echoes of other times they had felt let down and rejected. I also knew that a small minority, would be angry at losing the figure they loved to hate. Where would they direct their venom now? The thing that keeps some people functioning is having someone to constantly criticise and complain about. For some in my congregation, I had become the means by which they could continue to drip feed their discontent to the Bishop. How would they get his attention now? Lacking a suitable scapegoat might mean having to confront their own pain. Thankfully, I was still on a therapeutic journey and would be accompanied through this new phase of life. Besides, John knew, more than most, the impact these parishes were having on me.

Nevertheless, I discovered it is harder to leave a place that is difficult than one that has gone well. It was counterintuitive. I should have been delighted to skip off into the new situation I had been asked to consider, but I wasn't. I still had the drive to make things better, to rescue and redeem. My inner dialogue went like this: 'If only I could stay a little longer, things would turn around, they would see that I want the best for them, then I could leave.'

This is a childhood pattern. It is a longing for a past to be healed, an enduring reluctance to face the reality of what was, a resistance to working through the psychological pain that was buried as a way of coping. The Bishop's words came back to me: 'It is not going to change, Charmaine, and I would hate to see you ground down again.'

At the stroke of midnight on the eve of 2015, I ceased to be the vicar of my two rural parishes. Cinderella's coach had turned back into a pumpkin, there was no rescuing Prince Charming and the hope that had carried me into these parishes died.

I wept. The grieving began, and with it the sense of regret and failure. This prayer emerged; one I've used countless times for the bereaved.

You are tender towards your children
    and your mercy is over all your works.
    Heal the memories of hurt and failure.
    Give us the wisdom and grace to use aright
    the time that is left to us here on earth,
    to turn to Christ and follow in his steps
    in the way that leads to everlasting life.

Chapter Twenty-Two

BENEDICTUS

Vicarages are extraordinary houses. They are much larger residences than someone on a clergy stipend could normally afford to live in. They are multi-purposed. Expansive enough for a vicar and their family to occupy comfortably with a study that functions as the parish office, and reception rooms that can double up as parish function rooms. Each new incumbent of the vicarage is given a grant towards the cost of new curtains and carpets, and the cost of moving house is covered. This means that the joy of a full packing service can be included, a bonus when it comes to dismantling a study that is over full of books. I've heard a rumour that removal companies hate moving clergy because there is always a library of books to pack. The receiving parish agrees to decorate the vicarage while the property is empty, so that the hideous interior decorating taste of the former vicar can be dealt with swiftly. My preferences have always been for rooms painted with soothing off-white magnolia. I was keenly aware that this was all a luxury that will not be afforded for the last move I make, into retirement. But for now, I continued to enjoy living in a large, detached property with four bedrooms, two reception rooms and a study. Plus, a family bathroom, a downstairs cloakroom and, as the estate agents would say, ample room for storage.

However, a large question loomed. How would I continue to see my therapist, the new parishes were even further away, it would add at least an extra thirty minutes travelling time in each direction. I asked myself an even stranger question: 'Would I still be known in this new incarnation, in a different location?'

Most of the existing relationships are stripped away when a vicar moves, so I had a feeling that maybe this relationship would also be lost. One thing I wanted to do at the earliest opportunity was to phone John from the new house. So, one day, standing in an empty vicarage surrounded by the smell of newly laid carpets, John and I spoke on the phone. It would be ok, he assured me, nothing had changed, I was still known. I would just have to travel further for my weekly sessions.

Carpets down, curtains up, the day came for my induction as the new vicar of another two rural parishes. Or should I say, half-time vicar, as I was being paid just fifty percent of a full stipend. The Bishop and Archdeacon went ahead into a church full of people waiting for me. I was the last to leave the vicarage and, with a growing sense of apprehension, I made my way to the church. Unanswerable questions tumbled into my mind: What lay ahead for me now? What would this new chapter bring?

It was a dark, late January evening, and, as I entered the church, the organist was playing Karl Jenkins' 'Benedictus' from The Armed Man. I was taken back to the therapeutic space.

Many years earlier, this piece of music was on a CD that I listened to regularly as I travelled to and from my therapy sessions. As I had to drive some distance for my appointment, wanting to make the most use of the journey time, I listened to music. It was a great opportunity to feed my newfound love of country music. This song, 'Benedictus', was particularly haunting. The word Benedictus is an ecclesiastical term, an invocation or blessing, it is also the title of a prayer used daily in morning prayer. During one of our earlier sessions, when the work had started to become challenging, a silence fell in the room, and into my wordless mind came the music of 'Benedictus'.

'Where have you gone to, Charmaine?' John enquired. I was familiar with this intervention; it would often be used when I seemed to have gone somewhere else during our conversation or simply just withdrawn into myself. Where had I gone to? Sometimes I was visiting sadness, other times it would be anxiety or fear, or some other unnamed emotion that I either didn't recognise or in the early days lacked the confidence to voice. It took a long time to really believe that it was safe to say what I needed to say, that I wouldn't be judged, and my therapist wouldn't 'go off me'. This was the inner child craving approval from someone she admired. The words and music of 'Benedictus' played through my mind, it was soothing, calming and in response I answered, 'Benedictus.'

Benedictus –Qui venit in nomine Domini
Blessed is he who comes in the name of the Lord.

Who was this blessed one? Who was the one bringing blessing? Could it be both of us?

Would there be blessing in this new chapter? Was it a portent, a divine clue of more blessing to come?

Part Three

Chapter Twenty-Three

ART SCHOOL

Life as half-time vicar of two new parishes began, and the first challenge was to figure out how to do a job part-time when you live in a vicarage and the church's involved deserve and need someone working full-time. I was torn. I knew that I could easily fill my week working full-time. After all, this is what I had been doing for the past twenty-five years. I also knew that no matter how hard I worked, I would still only be paid on a half-time basis and there wouldn't be much more to show for my efforts. The parishes I had moved to had small congregations and lacked the critical mass around which growth might happen. It is difficult for someone to start attending church when the only service on offer is at 9.30 on a Sunday morning with a congregation of six. They were a very faithful six, devoted to their local parish church. Without them, the church would have closed long before I arrived. But it held little appeal to someone who might want to put in appearance anonymously to test the water of churchgoing.

This is a critical factor. When someone wants to attend church having either never been before, or not for a long time, they want to do it unnoticed. They have already battled various demons on the way, and overcome obstacles within and without. Among those critical voices might be ridicule from other family members. This, combined with an internal sense of not being good enough, means that going to church equates to a heroic journey. This situation needed much more than a half-time vicar.

I put this to the Bishop when I saw him for a six-month review. Though first, I thanked him for appointing me to this new post. It had been a good move.

'Well, Charmaine,' the Bishop began, 'people often find the only way to manage in a half-time post is by doing something else with the other half of their time.'

Already I could see this; we function in life as full-time people. So I would either do parish-related work full-time or attempt to do it part-time with the risk I would spend too much time watching daytime television for the other half of the time.

I wonder if the Bishop had in mind that I might do something 'worthy' with the unpaid part of my life. Maybe he thought I would take up a role as a counsellor again, and I considered this. It is difficult to function as a counsellor at the same time as being a parish priest, even though my own counsellor seemed to be managing this. There are always the tricky ethical issues surrounding dual roles. Confidentiality is an important element in a therapeutic relationship, which means someone living in my parish, coming to see me as a therapist, might feel compromised when they meet me in another context as the local vicar. Equally, such a person might be put off coming to church knowing that the vicar is also their counsellor.

I decided it wouldn't work for me trying to develop a counselling practice from the vicarage, though of course there would always be counselling elements in my role as parish priest, which I welcomed. I also recognised the need for something to take me out of the parish. It was time again to experience life where I wasn't known as the local vicar. I could maybe even explore my growing creativity. I was writing regularly and still performed as a singer at local folk clubs, but was it time now to try something new?

However, I wasn't quite ready for this statement from John as I walked into his office, 'You're an artist, Charmaine.'

I pondered this. Am I an artist? How did he know? Sure, I'd taken in some drawings into my therapy sessions, but did that make me an artist? Art making had become part of my process. There were times during the dark and difficult days of working towards healing when only images rather than words would work. The beauty of drawing with pastel chalks requires no skill to begin. I found it genuinely soothing and therapeutic to move, with a palette of many colours, across the paper using the flat of my hands to design shapes and gestures. The pain I couldn't express in words, written or spoken, found it's expression in simple abstract mark making. So, a regular practice was to see John on a Thursday and then spend the Friday attempting to process the work that was underway. Sometimes it brought relief, other times it intensified the emotion. I would lean into the polarities, feeling joy one minute followed by sobbing just a few minutes later. Internal storms were navigated until they found their safe harbour. Art practice had been part of my therapy, but could it translate into art education?

I decided to find out. One slow August day, with the words of my Bishop in mind, I started looking for something to do with the unpaid part of my life. I googled art courses. Several options emerged on my screen, including one closer to home than I expected. I found a course in art and design that I could do part-time at Wolverhampton Adult Education Service. Who knew that place existed? So, armed with my therapeutic artwork, I went for an interview with the tutor. No-one had seen my work before except John, not even Ian had seen it and yet here I was about to present it to a stranger and an artist! I was terrified.

Two more things were required as part of the interview. I had to take tests in maths and English. The reason for this was that the course served as an access to university, so the basic requirements for university entrance had to be satisfied. This was even more terrifying! I was confident about the English, after all I have a degree in theology and I use it regularly for work, but maths and I had long since parted company. Our last encounter was receiving my CSE grade four for maths in August 1970. The tests would also challenge my basic computer skills because they had to be completed online. I had absolutely no idea whether I could pass this maths exam.

When I received the offer of a place on the Art and Design course, I laughed hysterically. Partly out of relief because, to my amazement, I had been offered a place, but also because they were offering some additional support for my studies in English! It seems the maths was fine!

To start formal education again, at the age of sixty plus, in a completely new subject, was daunting. The confines of ecclesiastical life had become familiar, life as an art student pushed me way beyond my comfort zone. The other students were half my age and strangers. They were also already talented artists. I have often preached about the importance of expanding comfort zones and now it was my turn. This foray into a new adventure was scary. I shared my fears with my daughter. She urged me on and said, 'Mum, it will be good for you to do something other than vicaring.' Ian also lent his support as he had to so many of my previous crazy adventures. And the one who had almost booted me out his office to go to Nashville was equally affirming when I told him my plans. In a quiet voice he said, 'Well done.'

My weekly timetable expanded to include a drive to Wolverhampton twice a week. I began lessons in portraiture, ceramics, textiles and art history; all subjects that were new to me. The encouragement of my tutor kept me going. One lunchtime, a few weeks into the course, he came alongside and asked, 'Charmaine, why are you doing this course?'

The question took me by surprise, and I answered honestly, 'Well, I'm really doing it to get out of the parish a couple of days a week'. He continued, 'Most people do this course because they want to go to art school.' I paused; this had never occurred to me. A few moments passed before I said, 'Why, do you think I could go to art school?' Without hesitation he answered, 'I'm fully expecting you to.'

I was stunned. Could it be that this art tutor had seen something that only my therapist had named?

Was my labyrinthine pathway leading to this? It took a few days to consider before I was ready to go back to the tutor to ask how I should go about applying to art school, and to ask whether I should finish the course I was on first. After all, I was only in the first year of a two-year course. He told me that I would be invited for an interview, and I should take a portfolio of work along with me. Words were being used that had never been part of my vocabulary, words like 'portfolio'. So he set to work with me to create a portfolio of the artwork I had already completed. I still have that collection, I treasure it.

In September 2016, I enrolled as an undergraduate at the Wolverhampton School of Art, part of the University of Wolverhampton. Imposter syndrome, a constant companion, was keeping very close. Yes, the year at the Adult Education Service was intense and productive, but I still didn't think I knew how to draw and paint, which is what I thought art making was about. When I graduated from the University of Wolverhampton some years later, I used to mock complain to my tutors that they still hadn't taught me how to draw and paint!

The weekly routine as a part-timer was to travel to Wolverhampton School of Art, a brutalist building next door to the Wolves football ground in the centre of Wolverhampton. You can't miss it, although before I spent time there, I had missed it many times. If I had noticed it, I had had no idea what the building was for. It has seven-storeys, all of which are illuminated at night with multi-coloured fluorescent lights. They became a welcome sight of home, clearly visible when arriving at Wolverhampton train station. I had seen the light display many times, but still, it did not register then that this might be a place for art making.

Freshers' week was an eye-opener. By way of an ice breaker, our art tutors had all the new students working in groups. We were given the task of constructing a piece of art out of what can only be described as piles of junk spread around the seventh-floor fine art studio. The theme was 'Tension and Collapse'. It was a good descriptor for my anxiety levels. I was worried. The questions that flooded my mind were: What will they think of this old woman joining them? Who am I to be doing this? This was an echo of a couple of questions I asked myself decades earlier: Who am I to go to church? What right do I have to be doing this? I was crippled with self-doubt. For three decades my world had been my parishes, my churches; I was known as the vicar. Here I was in new territory, unknown, scared and not an artist.

On day three of freshers' week, I decided to stay in bed. I told myself I would return the next day. But I knew that if I didn't go back that afternoon, I would lose my nerve and never go back again. It was the classic 'fight, flight, freeze' reaction. I was ready to flee. But not wanting to be a university drop out within my first week, I got in my car and drove along the A449 to Wolverhampton.

But I was still a vicar, albeit a half-time one. Would there be divided loyalties? Well, for a while there were, until I started to realise that I was beginning to feel more like a priest in this secular institution of higher education than I ever had in my parish life. This surprised me, and it seemed as though as I shed the label 'vicar' it freed me to be who I was. It was refreshing to be among people who for the most part had not connection with church.

I wrestled with what seemed to be two separate worlds: the church and the art world. Was I parish priest or an art student? It felt like the classic dilemma of working mothers: when at work they feel guilty for not being at home, when at home they feel guilty about not being at work.

Adam, a student colleague and friend, helped me work this out. I invited him to visit my churches as I thought he would be interested to see the stained-glass window dedicated to St. Cecilia. It is a beautiful window, and unusual to have such a work of art in a small rural church. The window was a commission by modernist artist Keith New, whose work can also be found in Coventry Cathedral. As I was explaining to Adam, the symbolism of different artefacts and colours in the church. I was at the same time apologising for my lack of knowledge. I said, 'I'm not very good at this, it's always been a challenge for me being part of the institution. And because this is where I work, I don't really see it anymore.' His reply brought me up short with: 'Well, that would make a good art project!' Then he looked through the west window and continued with feeling; 'How can you not be inspired by this Charmaine? You don't realise how fortunate you are, most people don't have access to this kind of space.'

An idea came, could faith be accessed with an artist's eye? Might the baggage so many people carry about church be circumvented with art? I began to wonder what a 'cure of souls' might look like to an artist. Was there a way for my two selves to meet? And if so, how might they inform each other?

Art school became a twice weekly pilgrimage from rural south Staffordshire to city-centre Wolverhampton. As a group of would-be artists, we met with our tutors to discuss our ideas for art making. Most of my student colleagues were a good deal younger than me, younger even than my own daughters. It was an education in so many ways. These young, talented artists talked about their lives; they described the jobs they had to do because the days of student grants are long gone, and so they had to work as well as study. I learned a new vocabulary, and the unwritten rules of student flat sharing that cause havoc when broken.

During one tutorial, two young women looked at me and reflected how much easier it must have been when I was young. They wistfully longed for a time when a girl could meet a boy, almost by chance, and begin a relationship that would lead to a life partnership. Like it was in my day, they imagined.

I didn't rush to remove the rosy tinted spectacles because they went on to describe what life was like for young women today. I heard the horror stories of tinder and both women had given up going out to clubs because of the constant pestering from men. They felt like they were treated like commodities.

Chapter Twenty-Four

TUTORIALS AND GROUP CRIT

A stable of art education is the 'group crit.' This occurs at frequent intervals. My tutor would gather his students and take us on a tour of our studio spaces to look at each other's work. One student would describe their ideas as we looked at their work. We, in turn, then offered our opinion. It was nerve wracking, especially if the tutor was feeling provocative. I think the object of the exercise was to help us grow in confidence as we described our artwork, while at the same time to teach us to critique ourselves so as not to depend on the flattery of a viewing public. As we were all in the same boat, as we waited our turn to participate, we were inclined to be kind with our responses. Though, to be honest, it was hard sometimes to come with anything to say. The whole exercise put me in mind of preaching classes at theological college when we would nervously try out our embryonic sermonising skills.

But it was not uncommon for the group crit to end with at least one person in tears.

One time, I was that student. This time, it was not a group crit but a mid-term assessment with two tutors. Still doubting my artistic ability, I nervously introduced a painting I had attempted in the style of J.M.W. Turner. What I had wanted was warm appreciation of my efforts. It wasn't forthcoming. Quite the opposite; there was tutor silence. I was devastated. As the tutors walked away, I knew that if I didn't say something, I might not continue with my course. So, I asked if I could have five more minutes with Gavin, my personal tutor. I will be forever grateful that Gavin came back, and I promptly burst into tears. With loud sobbing I wailed, 'I feel such a fraud'. Gavin stooped down in front of me, his eyes locked with mine, and he said, 'Charmaine, you are not a fraud. Every art student hits a moment like this at art school.' He had heard me, and I started to understand the process. I was being asked what I was wanting to communicate to the world and how that would show itself visually. The job of my educators was to help me assess whether I was doing this effectively. My painting didn't have to look like a Turner, it had to express the things that mattered to me.

This was not the only time I asked myself 'why am I doing this?'

I doubted my ability constantly. In life drawing class I was in awe of what the other students were producing; in comparison my own work seemed inadequate. One day, my tutor helped me to understand what might be going on for me. With great insight he reflected that art school might be more difficult for me because I was used to being the expert in my working life. I had been a vicar for a long time, I knew what I was doing in that world, but here at I was a beginner. Added to that, my younger student colleagues had been learning how to make art for many years, often arriving with an A Level in art.

It was not pride, I did not think I should be better than them simply because of my age, I just didn't think I would ever be as good as them. So, I was constantly asking myself, was it worth trying? And what was I trying to do?

Because I was doing my degree part-time, I had six years to work it out. I was so thankful for this. How other students taking the fulltime route managed to complete the course in just three years was beyond me. It took me three years to even feel confident in the building, I was forever thinking that someone would stop me and ask, 'What are you doing here?'

I decided to follow my intuition and ask what I was curious about. In the product design department, there were always left over pieces of wood, off cuts from other projects. I hated these perfectly good pieces of wood being thrown out, so I started to collect them. The next idea I had was to explore the colour green. I don't particularly like the colour, but I started to think about associations with green. Jealousy, envy and sickness, being some of the negative connotations. Ireland, spring and growth, being more positive. So, I set about a project I called, 'Redeeming Green'. One of the more provocative tutors told me he like the title but questioned the idea of painting pieces of wood in different shades of green. I didn't care. This was progress!

Chapter Twenty-Five

TIME TO SAY GOODBYE

The day I had always dreaded had arrived. The ending of therapy.

John and I had spoken from time to time over the years about what the ending of our work together would look like. It was something that I could hardly dare contemplate, and yet it was an abiding fear. John assured me that when the time came, we would negotiate it together.

More than nine years had passed since I had first arrived one autumn morning to be greeted with the words; 'Tea? Coffee? The loo is in there.' We had covered so much ground; there had been psychological healing on a scale I could never have imagined, and I had already started to wonder how much work was left to do. The journeying had become tiresome and there was the continuing expense to consider. Even so, on the day John told me he would be moving, I felt as though I had run into a brick wall that had then collapsed upon me.

Circumstances had changed; John had been let down by

the ecclesiastical hierarchy so could no longer stay in his present position. He explained this carefully to assure me that I would hear that I wasn't the reason he was leaving. There were still many months to go before he left, and John told me this far in advance so that we would have time to end well. 'Ending well' is a psychotherapy term. To end well means that you don't just stop therapy, the same care is taken over the ending process as is taken at the beginning.

I knew this day had to come, but I didn't want it to end, and ending well didn't mean it wouldn't be painful. My weekly visits to a therapist had become part of my support structure. This was the place where I could be totally honest, where I could be myself. This had become more than therapy; it was a place to be mentored, somewhere to take tricky parish and pastoral problems. John was more than a dispassionate arbiter; I knew he was on my side and would see things from my point of view. That didn't mean he always agreed with everything I said, and over the years, he certainly challenged me. But he always seemed able to understand why I was the way I was and why I said the things I did.

Although the end date was still many months away, I started to count down the remaining sessions with a growing sense of panic and anxiety. Everything in me wanted to run away, to avoid the inevitable. I felt sad. I couldn't see how I was going to manage. Occasionally, John would gently chastise me, telling me that it was time to spread my wings and fly. Even so, there were times when I would be so angry. One time I was so angry with him that he was stunned into silence. John hadn't seen it coming. For a while, I was worried that I had finally blown it. But even then, he assured me that he would be ok after a few minutes, and that it was a good thing that the anger had been brought into the therapy space. I was reminded how often the therapist was able to do this – bring something positive out of what had just happened. I saw, maybe even for the first time, that this work had been costly for him, too. For the longest time, I had lived with the illusion that however I presented in the therapy room, it had no impact on him. In those minutes when he was trying to compose himself again to continue with the session, he showed me how it felt to be on the receiving end of my anger. I could see the hurt and I realised then how devastating my anger could be. At the end of the session, I asked John how he was. He replied, 'I'm ok, tired and a bit bruised, but ok.'

I was thankful for his honesty and authenticity. Another time during this long goodbye, I asked John if he would miss me. Could he carry on beyond our sessions as though we had never met? That was my fear. His reply surprised me, 'I won't miss the trauma, it was touch and go in those early days.'

They say that the work in the end times of therapy can be some of the most fruitful work that is done. I'm not sure that was true for me, there had been so much that had been important and life changing. This was one more task to accomplish – ending. And we would do it together. I had one last anxiety, where was John moving to? It mattered to me that I knew where he would be. I didn't know how he would feel if I asked him. John showed me the house he was moving to and gave me his address telling me that it would not be ethical for him to just move without my knowing where to. He had become more than a therapist. John had been a mentor; a confidante and he would continue as a friend.

Days after our final therapy session, the strangest thing happened. I became terribly ill. First, there was a flare up of something that had been niggling for some time. My gall bladder became very painful and the need to remove it became urgent. It was as though the pain I had been working through at a soul level made its final exit through my body. Thankfully, the gall bladder removal was straightforward. I took some weeks off work, but looking back, I never felt entirely better, and the reason why became apparent soon enough. The gall bladder problem triggered an episode of acute pancreatitis.

Ian called an ambulance, and the paramedics administered a dose of morphine before whisking me off to hospital. I had never been in an ambulance before, neither have I ever felt so ill. A weary Accident and Emergency doctor took over my care, confirming a diagnosis of pancreatitis. I was shocked that he wanted to admit me to a ward. He was surprised that I was considering going home. 'Do you feel well enough to go home?' he asked. I replied, 'Yes, but then again I have had some morphine for the pain.' 'Quite,' he said, 'and you haven't got morphine at home have you?' I hadn't. Eventually, I was admitted to a ward, and I have never been more grateful for free healthcare. As I watched medical staff attach each new drip or administer yet more pain relief, I gave thanks that it wouldn't mean I faced a bill for every item on my discharge from hospital. Still, I didn't realise how ill I was.

I needed to let my art school tutors know that I was in hospital as I would miss some elements of the course. In a whimsical moment, I emailed my tutor to ask what artwork I should be making about this experience of pancreatitis. Art school loves a concept. His reply was sobering. I had forgotten that my art tutor at that point, Simon, used to be a staff nurse in the NHS, and he replied, 'If you have pancreatitis, Charmaine, then you are very ill indeed. The thing you need to focus on is getting better!' I was seriously ill, and it helped to know that. It was as though I had been given permission to feel the way I did. When I finally returned to art school, I told him how helpful his comment had been and that he was the only one who could tell me how ill I really was. I asked him, 'Why didn't the medical staff tell me that.' Simon answered, 'Well, Charmaine, we generally take the view that if you're in hospital you will know!'

It took several weeks to fully recover, and I needed a long period of sick leave from my role as vicar. This gave me time to consider the years that had gone before and to ponder what might lie ahead. In a strange way, it was a bit like having another sabbatical. For a long time, I wondered if I would ever feel entirely well again. Would my energy return? And what about my ministry? Was this now the time to consider retirement? I felt burnt out.

The problem was that retirement itself would require energy. Like most Church of England clergy, on retirement I would have to move house, away from all that had become familiar. The question was, where to? For more than twenty years, we had lived in a vicarage, a size of house we would never be able to afford, so downsizing was inevitable. It was easy to put off making a final decision, and I did, for a while. After several weeks of rest and recuperation, I felt energised again, and ready to return to parish ministry. I had begun to prepare my sermon for my first Sunday back, it would be about new beginnings coinciding neatly with a baptism service that was planned.

Then two days before I was due back at work, I received an email from the Archdeacon. I may have mentioned already that emails from Church hierarchy always alarm me, this one was no exception. The Archdeacon was sending me a copy of a complaint she had received about me with her reply. The complaint was that I had not responded to a baptism enquiry. I knew the complainant well. I had conducted her marriage service, and I had noted her request making a mental note to attend to it as soon as I returned to work. The Archdeacon's reply to her was kind, saying that perhaps the reason for the delay was because I was on sick leave. The reply came quickly: 'But Charmaine is very active on social media!'

My posts to social media were my attempt to stay in touch with my parishioners and let them know my journey towards recovery. There was also an element of not wanting to be forgotten. She saw them because she was a Facebook friend.

I could understand this young mother's agitation. My experience of therapy gave me an insight into what seeing me on Facebook, whilst unavailable to her, would have triggered. I suspected she felt abandoned and unseen. I resonated with this. But for me it was the final straw. I knew I could no longer tolerate my vulnerability to attack. Try as I might to maintain my boundaries and strengthen my resilience, whilst showing compassion and pastoral care, I had had enough.

Chapter Twenty-Six

LEADING

LEAVING

R etirement planning started in earnest, and we began the search for a house. Meanwhile, my journey through art school continued, so wherever we lived I needed to be in reach of Wolverhampton School of Art to complete my Fine Art degree.

Winter 2020 and it was time for the dissertation. The angst in every undergraduate's education focuses on the need to produce evidence of their learning. For me and my art school colleagues, this evidence was to take the form of a dissertation on a specific piece of research. I decided to reflect on my journey towards and beyond ordination. As I considered the role of women in the Church, I would also evaluate the place of women in art history. My dissertation would be an exploration of the soul, spirit and gender in the art of two women artists. One of the women was the Italian artist Artemesia Gentileschi who hailed from the 16th century, the baroque era, and the other was Swedish artist, Hilma af Klint who was around in the early part of the 20th century, the earliest years of abstract art. I had the idea, so all I needed were the requisite five thousand words, bibliography, reference list and images.

I was eager to champion the two women artists I had selected. Hilma af Klint and Artemesia Gentileschi had both been successful artists in their time, and had both been forgotten, only now being rediscovered, and celebrated with retrospective exhibitions. I found a strange comfort in learning that the Church was not the only institution that had been tardy in allowing women to take their place as equals. In 2014, twenty years after we had been admitted as priests, the Church of England General Synod voted to allow women to become Bishops. On 26th January 2015 the first woman to be consecrated such was Rev Libby Lane. In 2019, a self-portrait of the brilliant artist Artemisia Gentileschi was bought by the National Gallery. Good news, until you realise that it is only the twentieth painting by a woman artist acquired by a gallery whose collection comprises 2,300 European paintings.

Sunday 27th December 2020 was my last Sunday as a parish vicar. The pandemic, with its latest lockdown, meant that my retirement party was a gathering of twelve socially distanced parishioners congregating in a chilly but sunny churchyard to toast thirty years of my life as a vicar. I was touched that my church wardens had made the effort to give me a send-off, and if I'm honest, part of me was relieved to be excused a big party. I think I was in denial that I was going to have to pack up and move out of a large, detached, four-bedroomed house, with its endless capacity for storage, into a three-bedroomed semi-detached house fifty miles away. The saving grace of the new house was, first, it had a room that could be used as an art studio, and second, it was affordable. We had already learned that mortgage companies don't like to lend to customers who are in their seventh decade.

The second round of lockdown meant that the house purchase and subsequent relocation was delayed. But in April 2021, a date for moving finally arrived. A vicarage study full of books had been whittled down to the essentials, while surplus furniture found its way to charity shops, friends or the local tip. We learned quickly what was acceptable for donation to charity shops, and what was not.

Days and weeks passed, buying curtains, carpets, more furniture, and simply getting used to not having a garage but having near neighbours. Both were unfamiliar to us. Unfamiliar, too, was the growing sense I had of feeling like a stranger in my own life. We had moved a few times during my life as a vicar when I had changed jobs, even to Paris. The change was always stressful. But although new parishes offered a fresh set of people to get to know, I was still the same, and so was the agenda. I was still the vicar, I knew my role, place and what was expected of me. This move was different. Now I was to be a stranger in a strange place; there were no automatic routes into this new community. Who was I now? Over the years, I had sometimes become frustrated with always being related to as the vicar, but at least it assured me a place in the community if I wanted it. I was alarmed at how traumatising I was finding this. Old insecurities emerged, of not being seen or known. Fortunately, there was still John on the end of the phone, who had made his move into retirement two years earlier. He told me that he had underestimated the impact it would have, and he helped me make sense of what was going on in my psyche. For years, carrying all that came with being a vicar, shaped my identity, so when it went, huge questions surfaced. Who am I now? Have I made a mistake? Why did we choose this house? These are just some of the questions that flooded my brain.

Then there was the tiredness. For what seemed like an age, I was so weary, I fell asleep unexpectedly at odd times during the day. It felt much more than the natural tiredness of a house move. It was as though the exertion of decades was taking its toll: the loneliness, the heartache and the heavy cost of pastoral care; all the things that had been held aloft came tumbling down.

Slowly as we made the house our home, things began to settle, and it was time to start my final year at art school.

I began the daily commute to Wolverhampton, this time by train. It was different. The station at Leamington Spa is a delightful example of Art Deco design. Styled on the travelling habits of the 1930s, there are posters of seaside destinations, cosy waiting rooms and a garden. Yes, there is a garden, neatly tended by local volunteers. The autumn sunshine cast shadows from the bicycle rack, giving an air of an abstract painting. The novelty of this new experience stimulated me, and the visual stimulus nourished my artistic soul. I took plenty of photographs of shadow patterns, autumn leaves and passing trains. I knew that somehow this new visual information would find its way into my art. But how? A graduate exhibition must be more than a collection of photographs of a local train station, albeit one that is Art Deco.

I had a heightened sense of place, and although I was familiar with Wolverhampton, my route there now was different. Besides this, the return journey took me to a home that was still new and unfamiliar. This unfamiliarity was good for me as a creative, and there is an expression that goes: 'Life begins at the edge of your comfort zone.' I was way beyond my comfort zone and somehow it was breathing new life into me.

I had retired from being a vicar, moved to a new location and was now journeying to art school differently. I wanted to mark this transition, to reflect upon it and somehow make art from it. It was time to talk to Dean, my new art tutor.

Chapter Twenty-Seven

A JOURNEY WITHOUT MAPS

It was also time to decide what to do for my final art project, the one that would lead to my graduate exhibition and contribute to my final mark.

I fancied doing Jackson Pollock style abstract painting on a large canvas. So, with mop in hand, I made large, multi-coloured, gestural marks. I was intentionally journeying with the paint. It felt visceral and energetic. There were more over-sized paintings to come. I wanted to make the most of the spacious luxury of this final-year studio space. I also wanted this final chapter of art school to represent my current experience of leaving one life and moving into another, even though the new life was still unknown.

I returned to a familiar theme, the labyrinth. A labyrinth presents a pathway to follow, step by step, with no clear view of how to reach the centre. All you can do is take each step and trust.

Over the years, walking a labyrinth had provided a

metaphor for my life. In the busyness and challenge of daily living, we often don't have a grand plan or clear destination; we just keep going one step at a time and trust. Cooking the next dinner or doing the weekly laundry become the steps that take us through our days and weeks. Sometimes our lives are filled with vision and exciting plans, often it feels like we are moving through fog. I wanted to express this visually in a way that also had hope.

Dean, my final year art tutor, had an almost mystical way of helping his students make art. His style was laid back. With tutorials that were conversational, he would somehow make sense of the words you were putting together, and then suggest an idea. At the conclusion of one such discussion Dean said, 'So, it sounds like place, journey and identity are important to you. How about painting on maps?' I hadn't thought of that. A job lot of maps were sourced later that day, from eBay. Next, I suggested, 'What if I wear my liturgical robe and film myself walking, as though I was walking away from something, in a performance piece?' Dean replied, 'You could make a robe out of maps!' 'Great idea,' I countered, 'but you're assuming I would know how to do that!'

The creative cauldron was starting to bubble with ideas. I couldn't make a robe, but I could make a stole. Our house move had unearthed a cache of long forgotten embroidery, made many years earlier. A role of organza was spotted at the local charity shop, silk paints were rediscovered. It all resulted in silk painting a map on organza, with abstract embroidery to highlight the way random roads take us. It lacked one final element, the labyrinth.

I wanted to film a performance piece of me wearing my clerical robe and newly created stole while walking a labyrinth. There was only one place to do this, and that was The Sheldon

Centre in Exeter. This was the place where such an important part of my therapeutic journey had been launched, a decade earlier.

With expensive camera equipment on loan from the art school, I drove to Exeter. Ian came too, to be my art technician. Day by day we would set up the equipment, I would walk the labyrinth and he would monitor the cameras. The trouble was, he would keep forgetting to keep quiet! So, Ian would hum to himself, or cough, not realising that all of his noises were being picked up by the sound equipment. Stern words were exchanged.

What I imagined would be an ethereal experience caught on camera, turned out to be much harder task to accomplish. There were takes and retakes. Viewing the net result on screen revealed my rear view. You don't often see yourself from behind, and it took a while to get over the shock! Nevertheless, eventually we got there, and it was a proud moment to be able to exhibit my graduate art project, A Journey Without Maps. In a generous studio space with walls painted the colour purple, my film ran on a loop. There were three screens, the two outer ones showing me walking the labyrinth from two different perspectives. The songbirds waking up for spring provided nature's soundtrack. I joined in with a central screen showing me facing the camera and singing:

Take this moment sign and space,
   take my friends around,
   here among us make the place
   where your love is found.

Around the walls of my exhibition space were silk drapes, painted and embroidered to resemble maps.

In September 2022, I graduated with a Bachelor of Arts (hons) First Class in Fine Art; It felt like the best thing I have ever done. It was the fruit of a therapeutic journey.

Was it a divine plan that I should be among the first women to be ordained priest in the Church of England? Or was I just in the right place at the right time, a kind of quirk of history? I could have never foreseen how the future would unfold. To become one of the first women priests was neither sought nor a reward for good behaviour. It was a grace, given. And becoming an artist, it was never even a dream.

It had all been a journey without maps, it still is.

Deo Gratias.

POETRY

These poems emerged around Easter time as I reflected on the meaning of Good Friday and Easter Sunday.

GOOD FRIDAY

It was a good Friday the day she began to realise
the ground beneath her feet was solid and that she was safe.
It was a good Friday when love was in the field and
shame no longer figural.
It was a good day when she woke to find her heart was light
For she had found someone who was her saving grace.
And she could say more about Good Friday,
redemption, salvation, sin and death defeated,
but she has no need, for she knows now about
self-giving love because of a self who gave
And in her understated way she is so thankful.

Good Friday 6th April 2012

The importance of naming. Mary Magdalene recognised the risen Jesus when he said her name. She both knew him and she knew herself.

FIRST FIRE

The Long night of darkness gives way to
the new light of dawn.
Daybreak is painted with a soft palette of
blue, red, green and gold.
There is relief and release – joy even
for a stone is rolled away,
and like the first fire of Easter
she knows resurrection.
Then she remembers her name.
She remembers her name as it is spoken
by the one who loves her.
She remembers her name when she hears it
in the voice of the one she loves.
and in that hearing lie hope, healing, gift, grace and beauty
in that hearing she remembers she is called by name
Eastertide

9th April 2012

Besetting thoughts for me were around the question of whether I was enough or not. Would I be acceptable only if I was interesting or entertaining? Would I be interesting enough as a client?! So I asked these questions in this poem using the language of therapy.

AM I ENOUGH?

Am I enough for you?
am I enough if I don't sing and dance?
if I don't cry and regress?
What if I don't need to know anything more about confluence
or
Parent, Adult, Child?
Am I enough for you then?
Am I enough if I don't sparkle with wit and insight?
Am I enough if all I need is love?
am I enough if all I need is you?
am I enough if I don't need anything, I am just me?

23rd June 2011

This poem emerged after a dream about polar bears! They were getting in the way, keeping me stuck in the same place. Then I reflected that residing at the polarities of extreme emotion can also get in the way.

BI-POLAR EXPRESS

Polarities lie dormant
if things
are safe and confined.
They cause no trouble
if left undisturbed.
So, she dwells in the shadow of safety
a world of enclosure and entrapment
but, she is no longer content to dwell there
taking the risk
she is looking for escape
and a chance to break free.
It is then that the polarities
like polar bears
become restless,
performing a rhythmic dance of distraction
and potential destruction
until she resigns and relinquishes her agency.
However
These days as the terror subsides
These ursine creatures are learning to settle.

14th May 2012

This poem came to me when I was driving home from a therapy session as I reflected on the subject of Transference.

BRAIN FREEZE

When I sit like a rabbit in the glare of headlights
or freeze like a computer screen overloaded with data
it is because there has been
signalling error
a system shutdown
a neural pathway derailment.

Earlier experience has been evoked
of a sergeant major issuing orders
commanding troops
bullying.
I think they call it 'father transference'.
But there was nothing 'fathering' about those times
just yelling, telling, hitting, hating and cruelty.
And I know you are not my father
I know your desire is to heal not harm.
But in those moments, minutes, hours of 'brain freeze'
I forget and cannot access your tenderness
it is deleted or rendered 'junk mail'.

24th March 2012

One Saturday afternoon was spent feeling miserable and lonely and hurting following the letter received, pointing out my mistakes.

SOMATISING

My body aches with the symptoms of stress.
Weariness of wounding and shortness of breathing
my body aches with the symptoms of stress.

My mind hurts with the lack of self-worth.
eyes that are streaming and soul that is scorching
my mind hurts for the lack of self-worth.

My being longs for the one who seems lost
love that is grieving and heart that is breaking
my heart longs for the one who is loved.

Please forgive me for mistakes that are made
Tell me; 'to err is human,' it's ok to be wrong
life is not over, that wisdom is gained
and I am still worth loving even when I'm mistaken.

24th November 2012

Sometimes a sigh from someone listening can communicate so much.

HEAVEN'S BREATH

Light as a feather
a healing sigh
brushes her soul
whispering
softly
'You are not alone
and it is safe now
from the storm.'

10th September 2012

...be merciful to me O God because I come to you for shelter
in the shadow of your wings I find protection until the raging storms are over...
Psalm 57

WHAT IS INTIMACY?

Intimacy
Like the gossamer thread of a spider's web
in turns both strong and fragile
is intimacy.
It is the love language of meeting
the sacred space of receiving and giving
sacred and scary.
But she, a linguist, does not yet know this language
finds it hard to learn and much is lost in translation.
So, she does need a good teacher.

22nd March 2012

Reflecting on a new-born left without 'gaze' when faced with therapeutic gaze later in life.

THERAPEUTIC GAZE

No-one looked so
without loving gaze
she lay alone unseen.
Now when you look there is
thrill and threat
hope and fear.
Wondering what you see,
she is confused and cannot read the signs.
So hides, avoiding rejection
forfeiting invitation.

26th March 2013

In 2019 I was on an art school trip to the Venice biennale.

*Crisis in Venice hotel, flooding, power cut, noisy hotel staff who
tell me when I ask them to be quieter: 'this is not a normal night,
this is a noisy night.' This was after I went downstairs to ask
them to be quieter. The look on the face of one of them told me
that this was serious, and they too were wondering how to cope in
the face of this power outage and rising sea water sweeping
through reception.*
End of journal entry.

I also wrote a poem/blessing for Venice – PAX VOBISCUM.
One of my student colleagues on the trip has a similar Roman
Catholic background to myself. She, like me, is of the age
where we were schooled in the mass in Latin. Though she is
not a practising Catholic or even a believer anymore – one day
she said to me 'Pax Vobiscum' and without hesitation I replied;
'Et cum spiritu tuo.' Who knew that was still in the memory
banks?! And so this emerged.

PAX VOBISCUM

PEACE BE WITH YOU **V**ENICE
AS YOUR
XENOPHILIA IS
VIOLATED BY
OCEAN
BREACHES AND FLOODED
INNER
SANCTUARIES
CRYING OUT FOR
UNCTION AND
MERCY
PAX VOSBISCUM
ET CUM SPIRITU TUO

16th November 2019

Anticipating my sabbatical to the USA.

FANTASEA BLUES

I wish I could sail away with you
far across the ocean blue
in a beautiful boat just made for two
I wish I could sail away with you.

I wish you would come away with me
far across the bountiful sea
to a land beyond psychotherapy
I wish you would come away with me

I wish you would take me away from this
lonely place to a land of bliss
the rainbow's end and the crock of gold
Let's leave now before we're too old.

11th June 2013

There was a poetry competition at Lichfield Cathedral. The theme was 'Light and Dark' – so this is on that theme. I didn't win but it was a good prompt to write.

LIGHTEN MY DARKNESS

Lighten my darkness
Penetrate the shadows of my mind
the dark recesses of this aching heart.
With the light of a thousand spinning stars
whose light extinguished long before I was born
stretch across the span of years
and penetrate the gloom.

Lighten my darkness
Friend and lover
Whisper warmth and welcome
draw alongside with your cheerful ways
Find in me the divine spark buried beneath
a morass of longing.

Bring light out of darkness
Let there be no more wasted years
or tears in hiding
Lead through the night to soft light dawning
Yet do not dazzle lest it become blinding.

23rd September 2019

On the same theme, but this time thinking of the sun and moon as non-identical twins, and my granddaughters Hope and Eowyn also non-identical twins.

NON-IDENTICAL TWINS

Night and day twin sisters of contradiction
Polar opposites of light and shade
Can either exist without the other
When both are birthed from mother earth
Is one preferred, a favoured child
She of extrovert disposition
The other sulking in her quiet contemplation.
Yet grace resides in gift of difference
Flourishing as darkness gives way to light
Who allows in turn night to give day rest.
These non-identical twins belong together
They wrap around like embracing lovers
Paradoxical companions of
Chalk and cheese, water to wine, breaking of bread
Even death and resurrection.

25th September 2019

Written in response to a visit to Falling Waters National Park, Florida, towards the end of my sabbatical March 2014. There was a waterfall and as I watched it I noticed a rainbow forming over the water.

DANCING IN THE RAINBOW

I'm dancing in the rainbow
With droplets of moisture
Gold and purple
raining, refreshing.

I'm breaking bread
sharing fragments
to feed those who hunger
with manna from heaven.

I'm pouring wine
satisfying souls
who live with yearning
and long to be met.

I'm woman at the well
drinking deeply
to quench an eternal thirst.
Shower on, life giving water.

November 2017

There are many ways to interact with or respond to a piece of art. These two poems *The Numinous* and *Epiphany,* emerged as my response to seeing two paintings by Dr Simon Harris at Wolverhampton Art School.

THE NUMINOUS

Black and orange turning to antique gold
Combine to evoke the numinous.
Hinting at things unseen
They dance to conceal and reveal
Unearthly presence

Stand still
Pause, breathe,
become aware of ethereal beauty
Allowing even your shadow self
To emerge and be bathed for a moment
With blessing.

13th December 2019

Viewed on 7th January 2020, the Orthodox Church Christmas Day is informed by the season of Epiphany celebrating the journey of the Maji to visit the infant Jesus and by the current sabre rattling and threats of war by Iran and the United States.

EPIPHANY

Do you see what I see?
A revealing or reflection?
At the dawning of the decade
In the season of the wise
Travellers still follow the trace
Hoping to find new artistry.

While the East still gives up her sons
To the tyranny of latter day Herods
Journeying souls long for reconciliation
A prince of peace instead of war.

Are we seen because you seek
Our beauty held in the beholding
and loved because you gaze?
Will 20-20 vision be manifested
by an Epiphany removing
the cataracts of complacency
clouding cynical complicity?
Do you see what I see
Or something better?

8th January 2020

EMPTINESS

One day as I was preparing to lead the Sunday service, I became aware that I didn't feel I had anything to offer. With nothing to encourage the faithful, I simply offered my feelings of emptiness to God.

All I have to offer today is emptiness.
So, I offer you my emptiness
Could 'my cup runneth over'
Become my watchword?
My emptiness transformed by your fullness?
But that is a future hope
Today all I have is emptiness
All there is to give
Not even a widow's mite of two copper coins
to grace this empty cup
Just emptiness

Palm Sunday, 25th March 2018

ASH WEDNESDAY

Ash Wednesday is the start of Lent, a purple season. People come for the annual imposition of ashes on the forehead for many reasons.

With ashened brow reminding of mortality
she bows her head and weeps.
Not for sin and desired repentance
but for love.
With soul shuddering sobs her body rocks
with rage and reckoning
assailed by waves of grief and anger
for there is no relief from this torrent,
this torment.
So she waits in foetal position
hatches battened down
praying for the storm to pass.

3rd March 2018

Reflections on the boundary of the therapeutic relationship and the metaphor of sailing into uncharted waters.

THE CORACLE

They sail in a coracle
not a rowing boat
nor a narrow boat
and certainly not a speed boat
but a coracle.
And, like the monks sent out by
St. Columba
they make their way to an
unknown destination.
The coracle is an unpredictable
vessel for transportation,
It has something of a mind of it's own
needing a skilful steer and expert handling,
like therapy really.
And within it's boundary is a circle of safety,
(though not without risk,)
holding and inviting trust.

21st April 2012

CHARMAINE HOST

THE JOURNEY OF THE WISE

It's a long and winding road
especially bleak this time of year.
Each twist and turn familiar
every passing mile measured
with motorway conveniences counted.

Travellers once were led by a star
a heavenly body whose destination revealed
the Christ child in the first phase of attachment.
As they were met on this holy ground
they were changed their continuing journey altered.

You are my guiding light
and I too am drawn still, seven years on
journeying to unlikely holy ground
meeting in the bleakness
illumination and food for the return.

16th November 2016

JERICHO

What if
she is good enough
to be:
wife, mother, friend, lover,
client, counsellor, prophet or priest?
Or even good enough to just be herself?
What if
she deserves:
laughter instead of tears, pleasure rather than shame?
Or even just deserves better?
What if
'not being good enough'
has been the cornerstone of her life's building,
the foundation upon which all her choices have been made?
What if
this stone is removed?
What will
the landscape look like when
these walls of Jericho come tumbling down?
What and how will she rebuild?

19th June 2012

About the Author

Warwickshire-based artist Charmaine Host was a parish vicar for more than twenty years, and on 23rd April 1994, she became one of the first women to be ordained as priest in the Church of England. In her writing and art practice she is interested in themes of spirituality, faith, personal growth and psychotherapy. Charmaine is also a therapeutic counsellor. As a writer, she has written countless sermons, articles for parish magazines, a dissertation and latterly poetry.

Her art practice includes abstract painting, textile work and photography. She also sings and plays the guitar, with an enduring love of country music and Nashville.

She is married to Ian and they have two adult daughters and twin granddaughters.

Purple into Gold is her first full length book.

A Journey Without Maps

The making of A Journey Without Maps
Wolverhampton Art School Graduate Exhibition

The final piece as was shown at the Fine Art Degree Show can be viewed here: https://youtu.be/cAIgiLdRdqc.

A Journey Without Maps began as a concept that would express spiritual journeying and moving on in life one step at a time. Labyrinths have become an important part of my spiritual journey especially the one located at The Sheldon Retreat Centre near Exeter.

The art work is a performance of me walking the labyrinth which was filmed with two cameras placed at two different angles. It marks my retirement from parish ministry, hence the wearing of a cassock with a handmade silk painted stole of hand-embroidered organza.

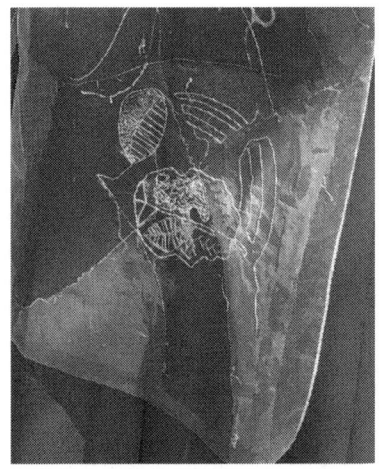

The hand-embroiled organza for the handmade silk painted stole.

A chartres style labyrinth at the Sheldon Retreat Centre, Exeter, Devon.

Acknowledgments

There are many people I want to thank for encouraging and helping me to write this book. Included among them is Michael Heppell whose masterclass I attended; it was both inspirational and a great motivator. It also introduced me to 'the emerging butterflies' my wonderful writing group who urged me on with suggestions, encouragements and kindness. Our meetings on Zoom spanned the length and breadth of England and Scotland, even including several points along the canal system.

Thank you, Debra, Lis, Judith, Erika, Mark, Jane, Elaine, Sam and Pen. I wouldn't have done it without you.

I have reflected on my thirty-three years of ordained ministry and were I to do it again, I hope I would have more grace and wisdom! So, a huge thank you to the many faithful parishioners who have loved me, tolerated me, encouraged me, listened to my sermons, were baffled by me and forgave me. I know now how much grace I received from you.

Thanks are also due to all the staff of the Wolverhampton School of Art, especially those who have tutored me; Gavin, Dean, Simon, Maggie, Euripides and my very first tutors, Laura and Sarah. Both excellent and talented young women, they were just starting out themselves as art educators and were wise beyond their years. They were a blessing to this art student. As I mention in the book, gaining a BA Fine Art First Class was the best thing I have ever done.

Finally, my editor, friend and fellow art student Rebecca Collins. We got to know each other thanks to a shared art school trip to Berlin as we spent many hours walking, talking, wining and dining, and sharing stories of how to make the world a better place. We even sang 'Country Roads' together at Berlin Airport! It was my good fortune to learn that as well as an artist she is an editor and runs an editing and publishing services company, Arch Publishing Services. When I told her I wanted to write a book, she told me to go for it and offered to read various chapters as they emerged. Rebecca helped me believe that I could do it. She was there at the start of this writing journey, and I am so thankful that she has stayed the course with me. I couldn't have done it without you.

This journey as 'one of the first' would not have been possible without the loving support of Ian, my husband, who is an excellent cook, household manager, partner in ministry and devoted husband, father and grandfather. He continues to encourage me and all who meet him. I am very thankful for him.

Printed in Great Britain
by Amazon

29858075R00121